Coming In

Coming In

Gays & lesbians reclaiming the spiritual journey

Urs Mattmann

Foreword by Richard Rohr

WILD GOOSE PUBLICATIONS

English edition © Urs Mattmann, 2006
Translated from the original German by Urs Mattmann
German edition © 2002 Kösel Verlag GmbH & Co, Munich

Published by
Wild Goose Publications
4th Floor, Savoy House, 140 Sauchiehall St, Glasgow G2 3DH, UK
web: www.ionabooks.com
Wild Goose Publications is the publishing division
of the Iona Community. Scottish Charity No. SCO03794.
Limited Company Reg. No. SCO96243.

ISBN 1 901557 98 7
13-digit ISBN 978-1-901557-98-5

Cover image created by Wild Goose Publications,
based on a photo by Ran Plett

A catalogue record for this book is available from the British Library.

Overseas distribution:
Australia: Willow Connection Pty Ltd, Unit 4A, 3-9 Kenneth Rd,
Manly Vale, NSW 2093
New Zealand: Pleroma, Higginson Street, Otane 4170,
Central Hawkes Bay
Canada: Novalis/Bayard Publishing & Distribution, 10 Lower
Spadina Ave., Suite 400, Toronto, Ontario M5V 2Z2

Permission to reproduce any part of this work in Australia or New
Zealand should be sought from Willow Connection.

Printed by Bell & Bain, Thornliebank, Glasgow, UK

Contents

I dedicate this book to my wonderful life partner,
Emanuel Grassi.

Acknowledgements

First of all, I have to say a big 'thank you' to all the gay men and lesbian women who have inspired this book both by their writing and through the example they provide of people on a mature Christian spiritual journey: John McNeill and his partner Charlie, Troy Perry, Chris Glaser, Patrick W. Collins, Freda Smith, Jean White, Hong Tan, Neil Whitehouse and the late P. Josef Doucé.

In close solidarity I give thanks to my beloved partner Emanuel Grassi, with whom I have shared my life since 1986, for his support; and to Pierre and Catherine Brunner-Dubey as founders of the Friedensgasse order and community, who have strongly influenced my life's journey and inspired me with a vision for a contemporary mystic Christian spirituality. I thank my parents and grandparents for nourishing my interest in a path of faith in my childhood.

I thank the many worshippers in the Lesbian and Gay Grassroots Church Basel, the participants in my retreats and seminars in Switzerland, Germany, Italy, England and Scotland, and my Psychosynthesis clients, for sharing their faith and life experiences with me. I also give thanks to the men and women with whom I was able to lead retreats, especially Werner Valentin, Cassandra Howes, Stafford Whiteaker and Keith Sylvester.

I am grateful to Sascha Dönges, director of the Institute for Psychosynthesis in Basel, for all I learnt during my five-year training and for her review of the original manuscript and her critical and helpful comments that helped to shape it. I am particularly indebted to editor Winfried Nonhoff of Kösel Verlag in Munich, the publisher of the original German edition, for his extensive and fruitful collaboration and openness, and to Ingrid Fink for helping to negotiate publication of the English edition. I did the translation myself but was strongly supported by Michael Szönyi, so I thank him for his corrections and suggestions. I am also grateful to Wild Goose Publications for publishing the English edition, and to Sandra Kramer for her co-operation and valuable work as editor.

It has been a special privilege to have known Richard Rohr for many years, so I was overjoyed when he accepted the invitation to write the foreword to this book. It can now be read in the original English for the first time.

Foreword

by Richard Rohr

Avoiding the risk of a transgression has become more important to us than holding a difficult position for God, and it is this that is killing us.

Fr Pierre Teilhard de Chardin, S.J.

Surprisingly – although maybe not – the issue of homosexuality has become the test case and the contentious issue inside most Christian denominations today. It divides otherwise reasonable people, and they move into fear, accusation, and quick absolutes or Scripture quotes – on both sides – to settle the seeming dust. When we deal with the issue of sexuality and gender, when we appear to be tampering with the basic archetypes of male and female, everybody gets defensive or aggressive. It's a sure giveaway that we are dealing with something very important and very mysterious. We are on holy ground, which always both attracts and intimidates at the same time. So the first thing we must do is take off our shoes.

In other words, we must tread lightly and with respect for the other, no matter on which side of the issue we find ourselves. Fundamentalist assertions are just as bad as fundamentalist rejections. The true gift will be found in the middle somewhere, not by avoiding the struggle but by entering into the mystery of human love, and letting it teach us and stretch us, until we are finally capable of hearing God in all things – even those things that at first appear dangerous. We must hear both the experience of healthy homosexual love and the social critiques of those who are trying to preserve other social and spiritual values. Both have something necessary to say, and both are hard to hear from the other side. So keep those shoes off until you can tiptoe over to the other perspective, and even, if we can dare to imagine it, to the perspective of a good God.

Once other believers can see that gay men and women are concerned about the values of faithfulness, and are willing to preserve the normative value of heterosexual marriage for the sake of human life's continuation, many of their fears will be lessened. Once gay women and men can expect trust and respect from other people and from society, I think we can begin a civil and truly spiritual conversation. We are still in the early stages of creating that conversation and that climate. Remember, true spirituality is always telling us to change, and not giving us weapons to change other people. How different Christian history would have been if we had just learned that one simple lesson. But somehow the human ego was not ready for that much participation in the mystery of transformation. It is so much easier to spend our lives 'converting' others than to undergo the always painful task of personal conversion. It is more attractive to feel ourselves 'right' than to continually admit that we are also partially wrong.

After working with people as a priest for over 31 years, I have come to an extraordinary conclusion: we come to God not by doing it right, but by doing it wrong. This is obvious to me now, although it does not really become obvious until the second half of life. By then, if we are honest, we have seen the pattern in ourselves and in others. You understand mercy and grace by looking backwards. Looking forwards it is just a nice theory, but not yet 'good news'.

Why, then, are we so obsessed with the bad news of being right? Why do we spend so much time trying to concoct a worthy ego? Whether we are homosexual or heterosexual, can't we just 'hold a difficult position for God'? Jesus appears to be doing just that, as he hangs archetypally between the good thief and the bad thief on the cross – naked before reality. He also pays the price of hanging on this collision of opposites, and it seems very few are willing to join him there. The realm of true faith, liminal space as I call it, will always be 'narrow' and 'only a few find it' (Matthew 7:14).

Homosexuality is emerging as the issue that institutional religion finds itself structurally most incapable of resolving. It reveals, like nothing else, the very limitations of managed religion. Denominations have to please constituencies and donors; they have to appear mainline and 'solid' to maintain their religious credibility. They find themselves incapable of dealing with genuine mystery because of their penchant for grand universals. They must preserve their authority and never be caught without an answer for everything. And, worst of all, they find themselves more and more incapable of dealing with the exceptions (precisely where Jesus was at his best!) because they are intent on being normative. All of these concerns are actually legitimate and understandable, but fortunately Jesus suffered under none of these social constraints. Quite simply, he was able to speak the truth to each person – as they needed it, when they needed it, and in a way they could hear it. All for the sake of leading them into union with God.

Once we know this is our only goal, the process becomes less paranoid, less controlling, and much more hopeful. Looking backwards at history and at our own lives, we learn that God 'uses all things unto good' (Romans 8:28). It is almost the only lesson of the Bible. There are no superiority positions in the Bible, only broken people who are used by God in spite of, and often because of, their mistakes. Later notions of perfection emerged with mathematics, the only area of life where it applies. It is not a biblical concept at all, except when it refers to the Godhead itself; it never refers to humankind. The worthiness road is a dead end. Where is the cut off point from unworthiness to worthiness? All we can do is desire, hope, and ask.

So let's join the grand parade of being human, let's surrender to the purifying process of learning how to love. It is an identical process for both homosexuals and heterosexuals, and we are all losing valuable time by trying to resolve this 'love mystery' in our heads or inside our separate group. I used to think that the opposite of control was just non-control or giving up. Gradually I have come to see that the true opposite of control is, in fact, participation.

The Gospel does not ask us just to give up control. That would be too simple, and even an abdication of the necessary tension. It asks us to participate in the mystery of active loving. Here, we are never in charge; here, we live in a luminous darkness;

here, we are never sure that we are doing it right, and – even better – we no longer need to be sure. This is the 'difficult position for God'. And this is why it is called faith and not certitude.

I trust that this wise and needed book by Urs Mattmann will lead us another step toward just that kind of faith. May it give a hopeful future to both sides of this contentious issue, and may it raise up a new generation of gay men and women who can offer their profound gifts to a society that needs all the gifts it can get to survive.

Richard Rohr, O.F.M.
Center for Action and Contemplation
Albuquerque, New Mexico

One

Introduction

In its original edition, *Coming In* was the first spiritual book written in German which was aimed mainly at gay and lesbian people and their friends. There were theological books on the issue but they were not written from a spiritual perspective. The same cannot be said of the English-speaking world, as there have been several gay/lesbian spiritual books published in English, whether from a Christian perspective or otherwise. While working on the UK edition I thought a lot about what makes this book unique. It's not just another spiritual book on the homosexual issue. It is written from a deep mystical perspective – a Christian mystical perspective that has a great openness to other traditions. It is a book that explores theology yet is also highly practical, offering prayers, rituals and suggestions for living a spiritual life. It addresses the potential and the unique gift that gays and lesbians have to offer to the world. I try to present a vision for this movement of liberation, together with a cosmology of faith. A glance at the titles of the chapters will give the reader a feeling of the holistic approach I attempt to convey.

For many years I have been creatively involved with the monthly worship services of a local gay/lesbian ecumenical worship group, and since 1997 I have been facilitating retreats for lesbians and gays in Europe. At all these events I encounter many lesbians and gays who express a spiritual yearning. They are searching for a relevant form of faith; they desire to discover and travel their own spiritual path. As a result, there are many things to celebrate, but there are also many questions to be asked and issues raised.

With this book I want to demonstrate what a relevant and liberating spirituality can mean for gays and lesbians, and how this spirituality can enrich our lives on a practical level. In these chapters I focus on an open and deep Christian spirituality. Although I have entered into dialogue with other religious traditions and have therefore acquired knowledge about them and a flavour of some of their gifts, I continue to be firmly rooted in the Christian tradition. Following the footsteps of Jesus has given me the freedom to explore some of the aims of esoteric tradition, deeming some aspects problematic and others helpful. I am a gay man, a follower of Christ. In my personal opinion it is vitally important to feel at home in one tradition and thus be able to explore its complexities and its depths. I am also convinced that the Christian spiritual tradition has a lot to offer gays and lesbians. It must be said that, in spite of the often anti-sexual attitudes that have prevailed in the churches throughout the centuries, in no other world religion is there so much questioning, dialogue and breakthrough going on than in the Christian tradition.

The main emphasis in my writing is spiritual rather than theological. While this book does have theological implications, its central focus is the spiritual path. The great Catholic theologian of the 20th century Karl Rahner once said: 'The Christian of the 21st century will be a mystic or he (or she) will not exist.' I want to open the doors so that readers of this book can experience the Christian faith as a spiritual reality, especially gays and lesbians who have been rejected or even condemned by their churches. This book therefore does not lay out a new dogma for lesbian women and gay men but rather explores a Christian mystic spirituality rooted in one's own experience. All true mystic spirituality breaks through barriers of dualism and exclusion, so in these pages I have attempted to describe a spirituality that bridges, explores, liberates and reconciles faith and sexuality.

When I wrote the original German version of this book, I was living with my partner in a community where we had a small sanctuary in the house. Within it was my favourite icon which pictures Jesus with his arm around one of his disciples. Sitting on my meditation cushion, I always prayed facing this icon. I prayed with all aspects of my being. I was present as a gay man. I was silent. I spoke. I was full of attention and surrender. I started to feel within me this image of Christ holding a man. Christ spoke to me: 'I, Christ, am fully present in you. Your homosexuality is fully embraced in Me. Your being gay nourishes the Source in the depth of your being. Your sexuality enriches you and is a gift to the world. Your gayness opens up your consciousness.'

This book deals with the mystic journey undertaken by those who are sexually different: gay men, lesbian women, bisexuals. The point of these chapters is not to justify same-sex sexual orientation but to discover its purpose and to render it fertile by integrating it into spirituality.

To this interpretation of spirituality I also add some of my experiences of other religions and especially I include the wisdom of transpersonal psychology (mainly in the form of Psychosynthesis) and the gift of meditation (mainly Zen and Christian contemplation).

Even though I studied theology for two years at a biblical college, it was to a much larger extent my meditation experience that strengthened my understanding of God and experience of Christ. Of course this did not happen overnight. I have been following the meditative path more or less intensively since the age of 27. Psychosynthesis, a major school of the transpersonal psychology tradition, was founded by Roberto Assagioli, originally a student of Sigmund Freud. It is a branch of psychology that includes the spiritual aspect of the human being. I was privileged to receive a full five-year training as a Psychosynthesis guide and therapist. God used this training and my meditation exercises to allow me more fully to grasp what St Paul meant when he said: 'It is not I who live, but Christ who lives in me.' This dimension and experience of the reality of Christ has shone a new light onto my life as a gay man.

While writing this book I worked through quite a number of the many gay and lesbian spiritual books that are available, most of them written in North America. Some of the books are classics, like the ones by John McNeill or Chris Glaser; others, such as those by Toby Johnson, deserve to be better known. More titles are recommended in the bibliography at the end of this book. I have been inspired in my life by many of these books and some have influenced the chapters that follow.

In his important book *Gay Spirit*, Marc Thompson describes the major concern of the spiritual gay and lesbian movement by asking four questions: Who are we? Where are we coming from?

Why are we here? Where are we going?

It's fascinating to see how many people have answered those questions from a spiritual perspective. I was quite surprised and deeply moved to find that as long as fifty or a hundred years ago some gay men wrestled profoundly with and wrote about spiritual issues. Those four questions were raised by individuals like Walt Whitman, Gerald Heard and Harry Hay in North America, and Edward Carpenter in Britain. They developed a vision for homosexual people – Whitman less explicitly, but Heard, Hay and Carpenter gave it a name. Since 1970 the international gay and lesbian Christian movement has been blessed with more and more lesbians and gays who have stood out in their life and faith: gay men like the aforementioned John McNeill and Chris Glaser, and Troy Perry; lesbian women like Carter Hayward, Elisabeth Stuart or Virginia Ramey Mollenkott. I rejoice for the ministry these women and men have provided. Some were true pioneers in a homophobic environment; others are just discovering their calling and contribution. Their vision flows into this book and I have built on some of their ideas.

Something that I deem very important is the potential of homosexuality. This assumes that homosexuality is not an accident, a pointless product of creation, but that it makes sense and has a purpose. This purpose – and one might also add 'calling' – includes different and special gifts, qualities, responsibilities. These 'queer' gifts of gay and lesbian people are not only for use in their own personal development but also for service in and to the world.

A common error made both by enemies of the homosexual movement and at the same time by members of the gay and lesbian scene themselves is to reduce homosexuality to just sex. Certainly, homosexual intercourse usually goes along with being gay and lesbian and lived genital same-sex sexuality can be an important expression of our being and personality and may be a source of strength for lovers. But there are second and third levels or aspects of homosexuality.

The obvious second level is homosexuality in a relationship.

In a life partnership of two people of the same sex, a wonderful, loving union can develop in which sexual communion may constitute only a fraction of the time spent together. There is so much more to a shared life, including conversation, tenderness and common activities. Couples on a spiritual path together will be likely to take part in mutual prayer or worship or sitting in meditation together.

The third level has been given the least attention so far. I would describe this level of homosexuality as a different or altered kind.of consciousness. This hidden potential of same-sex love is what we shall be discovering and exploring in this book.

Along with considering the spiritual point of view, we shall also be looking at our gay/lesbian sexuality itself as part of a relevant Christian faith. How can sexuality become a source not only of joy but also of strength, nourishment and even revitalisation. We will also consider this dimension within the context of the culture of sexual consumerism which plays a significant part in our society. While lesbians might be more cautious about this tendency, many gay men are fully and uncritically involved in this hedonistic approach. Sexuality in our society is more often than not reduced to a product, an act that achieves a few moments of ecstasy. As a result, the choice of partner becomes less important as long as he fulfils my fantasies of sexual attractiveness and promises quick satisfaction.

How can we find new ways of dealing with our sexual drive with respect and integrity? I hope I will be able to provide some insights about a holistic approach to rediscovering our sexual energy as a source of strength. This journey will not exclude critical questions about the cult of youth that dominates sections of the gay scene – just as it also dominates other parts of society. Of course, it doesn't make sense to issue harsh, moralistic statements, or to impose simplistic bans that haven't been thought through. The way forward is an invitation to explore the options for a sexuality that is connected to soul, spirit and mind, as well as body.

As we go along, I will refer to my experiences as a member of an ecumenical order, the Friedensgasse Community, to which my partner and I both belong. This order will be introduced in Chapter 10, which looks at the possibilities for gays and lesbians to find a spiritual home.

I hope it has become obvious that I have written this book not as a neutral observer or from a detached, theoretical point of view. My Christian spiritual journey as a gay man underpins all that I write. This journey started consciously in 1978 when I was 18. That was when I started to come out and accept and appreciate my same-sex orientation. It was then that I took part for the first time in a gay and lesbian conference in a church seminar centre. In the same year – and this may be no coincidence – I underwent, by God's grace, a surprising and transformative spiritual experience in which I encountered God's love in a profound dimension that I hadn't known before and that showed me new aspects of Christ. It started one night with what I felt as a powerful 'explosion' of the divine spirit within myself.

My partner Emanuel Grassi, with whom I have shared my life since 1986, has played a large part in the creation of this book through all he has given and taught me throughout the last two decades. On the 8th October 1988 Emanuel and I celebrated our partnership in a worship service where our union was blessed and we were able to formulate our promises and intentions for this relationship, which we hope and expect to last our whole life. In Chapter 5 I will explore the spiritual issues surrounding same-sex partnerships.

I am aware that I am writing this book as a man and I know that there are some differences of outlook between gay men and lesbian women. Nevertheless, there are interconnections and there is common ground, especially when we look at our life journeys from a spiritual point of view. I decided that, as much as it was possible for me as a male writer, I would include the situation of lesbians. For over twenty years I have had lesbian friends and have worked with lesbian or bisexual women leading retreats and seminars, or have got to know them as participants or as clients in counselling. This has given me many opportunities to learn about our differences and our areas of agreement. Whenever possible, I try to use a form of language that includes both men and women, and there are passages where I make it clear that God is male and female and beyond both.

I am aware that in the English language there are other names for gays and lesbians, words that have no direct counterpart in the German language in which I originally wrote this book. One expression is LGBT which means LesbianGayBisexualTranssexual. I somehow have a dislike for acronyms and I hesitate to use this broad label all the time. It is, of course, very inclusive. But, to be honest, I haven't yet had as many close contacts with transsexuals as with the other groups. Still, I assume that some of the observations and conclusions in this book will work for all sexual minorities, including bisexual readers. In my contact with bisexual women and men I have found that we have many issues in common. Some of these depend on that person's choice of relationship – straight or same-sex. So, many aspects of this book will speak to bisexual readers, although they may find that a few things are not relevant because of different life circumstances.

The other expression is 'queer'. I kind of like this word. I like its sound. It is simple and includes gays and lesbians and, for many, also bisexuals. Of course, I am aware that for people who have grown up in an English-speaking country it may sound offensive and is reminiscent of times when it was used as a term of abuse. On the other hand, some progressive gay/lesbian organisations and books have reclaimed it – and recently it has been positively reinvented on TV with the popular programmes 'Queer as Folk' and 'Queer Eye for the Straight Guy'.

Some radicals call themselves queer because they have a not totally unfounded belief that much of the gay and lesbian movement has become too fully assimilated into mainstream society. The true – and commonly used until about fifty years ago – meaning of 'queer' is 'strange', 'different' or 'weird'. Some of these words could also describe aspects of Jesus, who was despised by the fundamentalists of his time. I will occasionally use the word queer. Think of this Jesus connection when I do so!

As I was working on the English version of this book, I got hold of a breathtaking sermon by Rev. Dr Penny Nixon, a lesbian minister of the Metropolitan Community Church in San Francisco. She gave this sermon just after the disturbing re-election of George W. Bush in November 2004. She titled the sermon 'From Strength to Strength or Be Queer for Four More Years' and went on [...]

> *So I have a challenge: Be a Queer for the next four years!*
> *I want us to be queerer than ever. Queer – not gay.*
> *We need to broaden our definitions of queer:*
> *Queer – means an array of genders, of families, of loves;*
> *Queer – means being suspicious of the status quo (without and within);*
> *Queer – means moving outside the norm where we are in solidarity with all the marginalised;*
> *Queer – means a persistent refusal to be assimilated;*
> *Queer – means an insistent authenticity, telling and living the truths of our lives.*

(From the January 2005 issue of the MCC Hamburg newsletter)

While I will use the word queer in the homosexual sense in this book unless noted otherwise, I think this great challenge puts the word 'queer' into a much more useful context.

I have translated this book into English myself and in the process have reworked a few aspects of it. For example, I have taken the situation in the English-speaking world into full account and have left out much that relates only to the German-speaking part of Europe. The emphasis is mainly on the situation in the British Isles but also in North America. I lived for one year in California in 1980-81 and twenty years later for over three months in England, south of Manchester. Over the years, I have travelled repeatedly to North America and more and more frequently to Britain before moving with my partner to England in 2005. When travelling through South India in early 2004, some Indian friends in Tamil Nadu told me they would like a Tamil edition of my book. Who knows, maybe India's next!

This is a practical book which gives specific suggestions and inspirations on how to put the ideas to work in your life. So you'll find plenty of examples of meditations, visualisation exercises, rituals and prayers. I hope this allows the vision of this book to become substance in your life.

I have been involved in facilitating, leading or making a contribution to worship services for the last quarter of a century. For ten years I was part of a team that organised and led experimental worship services in Basel, Switzerland, and for an even longer time I was actively involved in a monthly worship service for gays and lesbians in the same town. Since 1997 I have led retreats, workshops and seminars – the majority for gay and lesbian participants – every year. Through this I have been given the opportunity not only to develop guided meditations, rituals and liturgies but also to try them out. All this flows into this book, so in a way it has been many years in the making.

I hope that my book promotes and fosters the spiritual aspect of the LGBT movement in general. I believe, in fact, that a major leap in evolution is needed. But we are not starting from point zero. As I testify in these pages, many spiritual approaches – whether Christian or otherwise – already exist, although they are largely ignored by the media. At the end of the book I list the addresses of some exciting initiatives.

When I wrote the original German version in 2001, I did so partly in Basel, and partly in the spiritual centre in Tuscany of the order I mentioned. I especially remember the two weeks in the Podere Fiorli under the Tuscan sun. Buoyed up by the daily meditations and liturgies in the chapel, I felt full to overflowing with God's Spirit. I knew that this book had to be born.

Gay and lesbian Christians have fought for acceptance for the past four decades and there have been countless theological books and endless discussions aimed at proving that homosexuality is not 'sinful' as such. Now we need to change and broaden the emphasis. We have to understand that we are already church, for it is just as Jesus said: 'Where three or four are gathered together in my name, I am with you.' This church-creating process – this 'being in me of Christ', this' Christ being in us', our unity with the divine reality – not only empowers us but changes our perspective. In the end, the spiritual worth and growth of each of us is totally independent of the pronouncements of the Church, whether it is homophobic or encouraging on this or other issues.

In most western and central European countries, many urban areas of North America, parts of the Australian continent and a few other places around the world, some highly visible progress has been made. At last we have gained more rights. And there are more parties. Glancing at a commercial gay magazine sometimes gives the impression that there is an ongoing carnival. Celebration is fun – but what lies beyond rights and parties? As important as they are, is this all that counts? I am convinced that further steps have to follow. We are called to discover and invest our potential, our consciousness and our gifts to a larger and more dynamic extent. We need to invest it all into the well-being of creation in every way possible: struggling for justice and peace, saving the environment, enhancing the spiritual dimension of religion, bringing more creativity to the arts and the media, and healing and standing in solidarity with the afflicted. Our world needs what we have to give, especially at this point of crisis in the history of our planet and the human family.

May this book inspire you to a personal spiritual adventure! May it be a journey that challenges and supports – not just individuals but also queer spiritual groups. May it nourish those that exist and help jumpstart new initiatives waiting to be born.

I trust that heterosexual readers will profit from this book too, by understanding better the dynamics of the gay and lesbian spiritual path with its many issues. In fact, I have been getting feedback about the German edition from heterosexual readers and I am glad to learn that this book provides insights for all kinds of people. Heterosexual men and women also have to confront issues of faith and sexuality, of being wounded, of discovering their calling and gifts.

This book arises from a Christian cosmology where everyone

has his or her place. It is a book that invites you to dream. Those dreams want to become reality. New roads wait to be travelled.

> *If you want to build a ship, don't drum up people to collect wood and don't assign them tasks and work, but rather teach them to long for the endless immensity of the sea.*
>
> Antoine de Saint-Exupéry

Each chapter of this book ends with some questions, suggestions, exercises and prayers.

The **questions** are posed to help you digest the points covered in the chapter and relate them to your own life and goals. I hope these questions will stimulate a process of personal reflection and contemplation.

The *suggestions* are simple intentions and actions to follow up. They will help you to integrate the issues discussed in each chapter and, as a result, make adjustments in your daily life.

The *exercises* may be guided meditations, rituals, or exercises for the body or imagination. They will help you experience the subject of each chapter on a different level, with your heart and a deeper consciousness, and will aid you in opening up to your own unique process of personal growth. As you will see, some exercises need to be done with eyes closed. In this case it is necessary either to memorise the text or to record it onto a tape first; or to do the exercise with a trusted friend who respects your spiritual path. It is also important to prepare the space in which you do these exercises. Set aside enough time, switch off your mobile or even unplug your home phone – anything it takes to ensure that you feel comfortable in your surroundings.

The *prayers* invite you to bring before God in supplication, thanks and praise whatever is broken open. The prayers I have written can be complemented with your own words. I hope this will encourage you to pray in a personal way or to formulate completely new prayers. Maybe you will want to write these down. The prayers in this book are moulded by my personal background and faith journey and so I often use concepts from Christian spirituality and the Christian mystic tradition. If you come from another tradition, you can adapt these to your own religious background or psychological framework.

I urge you to keep an empty journal and a pen ready when reading this book. It is not an abstract and theoretical text. Its intention is to move, challenge and nourish you.

All the questions, suggestions, exercises and prayers in this book can also be very useful in a group context – in workshops, worship services, retreats, etc. In fact, I have used many of them in such situations.

QUESTIONS

Were any important expectations raised for you while reading the introduction?

How do these expectations connect with your daily life?

What image of God is most accurate and important for you right now?

Do you define yourself as Christian or are you connected with another of the world religions? Or have you been looking for a spiritual path outside any of the established religions?

Are you ready to embark on a spiritual process?

SUGGESTIONS

Contemplate your experiences of being queer and your spirituality up to the present.

Take some time to reflect on the yearnings and longings in your life. Maybe it would help to make a list of these.

EXERCISE

Meditation with light

This guided meditation invites you to open up to the spiritual dimension implied in this book by stepping into a process of awareness of your personal faith and sexual orientation. Its intention is to help you become receptive and consciously invite the mystic reality of Christ into your spiritual journey.

Choose a quiet place, and sit comfortably but upright in a good posture. Now re-read attentively the chapter titles on the contents page of this book and maybe part or all of the introduction as well. Then put the book aside and close your eyes. Become aware of your breath. Breathe deeply in and out to your own rhythm.

Now see yourself in your situation as a homosexual person, or however you describe yourself. Be aware of your same-sex orientation and feelings. Become conscious that you are a spiritual being. Be delighted to become aware of all of this!

Then see, in your imagination, the book *Coming In* lying close to where you are sitting in the room.

Now discover in your imagination a light, one or two metres above your head. It is the clear, bright, healing and loving light of Christ. Visualise this light entering your body through the crown of your head and slowly penetrating the rest of your body: from your head with its sensory organs, to your pelvis with your genitals, to your feet and your toes, and all that is in between. Step by step, picture this light filling your body. You have enough time to let this light encompass your whole body and also the essence of your being.

With your eyes still closed, turn your attention again to the book. See how this divine light also extends to this book and enfolds it. Be aware that the book is connected with you through this light of Christ.

Open yourself to a sense that Christ is guiding you on your journey as a gay man or lesbian woman and wants to open new doors to broaden and deepen your understanding of your sexuality, of being queer, and of your faith and spirituality.

Be aware that this light of Christ is always present as you read and digest this book and in all your various life situations. In this awareness, slowly open your eyes and become fully present in your room. Have a good stretch.

PRAYER

Cosmic Christ, I am in You, You are in me.
Guide me in this new period of my life.
Show me the greatness of my humanity,
the richness of my being gay or lesbian,
and open me to a new experience of my spirituality.
I thank You for Your all-encompassing love
which surrounds me and enters me.

Two

Queer Spirituality

Lesbians and gay men discover Christian mysticism

In this chapter I turn the spotlight on the coming together of being queer with being spiritual. To explore this issue we must look at what we mean by spirituality. Many people talk of spirituality nowadays but the meaning is not always clear. The word is used in many different ways, often with different implications. That is why, for the purposes of this book, I find it helpful to clarify what is meant by spirituality and being spiritual. Of course, in the available space it's not possible to explore fully all aspects of the meaning of these words, nor can I mention all my spiritual experiences! However, as an important aspect of this chapter I invite you to discover some of the riches of the Christian mystic tradition and outlook. I hope this will make you curious, so that you will want to explore this fascinating and challenging path further. In the mystic tradition of religion lies one of the keys to a relevant and meaningful spirituality for the present time, and even more so for the world's future.

Major concerns of spirituality

Twenty years ago I hardly knew the word 'spirituality' and yet today it's an essential word in expressing the central aspect of my life and faith. In my youth I only used the words 'belief' and 'faith' to describe my Christian religious experience.

For me, spirituality embraces faith, belief, piety and religion, and fills these things with life and holds them together. In other words, spirituality is the experience of the Divine in our lives. It is something that has to be experienced personally. Nobody can prescribe or command it. The experience of God in my life is something deeply personal, yet it has vast implications beyond my individual self. True spiritual experiences encompass humanity and nature, all of creation. Spirituality has to do with an experience of being one with all there is. It is not at all about avoiding differences or making everyone the same. The point is finding unity in diversity. It may express itself in being at peace with oneself, or in being aware of one's connection with all of creation and with God. This was something often taught by Jesus when he mentioned his being one with God and encouraged his followers to open up to the same reality. The parable of the vine and the branches is a beautiful example of this mystic language.

Spirituality includes an awareness of the life, energy and power that are within us. It brings us into contact with transpersonal qualities like joy, thankfulness, generosity and compassion.

My Christian background allows me to experience the Divine in me as the reality of the Christ within, striving towards the experience that St Paul described: 'It is not I who live but Christ who lives in me.' A Buddhist may call this reality Buddha-Nature and a Hindu may call it Atman. A Jewish Mystic or a Sufi Muslim will use yet other expressions. While I am personally convinced that, in the end, all these terms point to the same divine reality, I do feel that how we name and address this reality matters. It has major consequences for the way we live our lives, how we worship and express our faith, and the ethics of our lifestyle.

Using this approach, spirituality has – in contrast to some esoteric or New Age belief systems – something to do with a love relationship, with a love for and from God. For me, this means that God is not an anonymous energy but a loving You. In this 'divine beyond', this 'God the other', I enter a relationship that is not dualistic: God is in me, I am in God, and yet God is a loving You that embraces the universe. The Christian tradition expresses this as God-the-Father/Mother, Christ and the Holy Spirit. The Divine Mystery in Relationship. All the major world religions have a trinity concept of God, but none of them have expressed it so explicitly as has the Christian tradition.

Spirituality isn't something that can be limited by physical church buildings, temples or whatever other sacred spaces humans create. Real spirituality enters my daily life and expresses itself in how I care for myself, my neighbour and my environment. Spirituality broadens the consciousness. That is why in fundamentalist groups there is often little left of a healthy spirituality, even if they raise their arms in ecstasy or speak in tongues. 'Fundamentalist spirituality' is a contradiction in terms. A spiritual path widens one's horizons in life; it doesn't make you narrow-minded. The members of some esoteric groups, on the other hand, also miss the point by being too narcissistic. They are so concerned about their own inner growth that they ignore the severe problems that exist in the world and the action that is necessary to counteract such ills.

Spirituality obviously does have its personal growth aspect – you are reading this book after all! – but it calls forth an engagement with the world. Spirituality is both simple and demanding. A spiritual path calls us to live consciously, to live out of the spirit in us and to learn to discern what is life-enhancing and what is not. This process of discernment is important, as many spiritual aspects of life are trivialised and marketed or even abused. (Some cults operate on the level of spiritual abuse or exploitation. As consciousness scientist Ken Wilber, in his milestone books, has explained, there are groups who cannot differentiate between transpersonal experiences of unity in diversity with the divine and pre-personal, diffuse symbiotic experiences of the powers of the subconscious.)

Nor does a deeply spiritual path mean a life without pain or darkness. Spirituality is not only an experience of light and joy, as some would like to have it. It doesn't seek suffering but it doesn't suppress or deny it either. The experience of God is present in difficult times too. The spiritual path may open us up to the shadow and unauthentic sides of our lives. A spiritual life will encourage us to let go of destructive life patterns and false assumptions. It will lead us through darkness to the fullness of life. I often compare the rhythms of spirituality to a birthing process, with all that involves: pain, joy, letting go, fertility, devotion and a new life. (In the Gospels, Jesus hints at this idea with the call to be born anew. The meaning of his statement has often been misinterpreted and twisted into an abusive 'born-again' approach that demands blind belief, but still this call is of importance in understanding a spiritual life. It is an idea seen in other religions too.)

I want to continue by emphasising four paramount concerns for a spiritual life and journey:

First: Take time out to meditate regularly, to pray to God, to listen to your inner self and to practise and exercise your full awareness.

Second: Develop dialogue and friendship with other people on a spiritual path. Search for a spiritual community that supports you. Decide on tools (e.g. meditation courses) which enhance your spiritual praxis and choose good spiritual literature to read.

Third: Integrate your spiritual experiences into your daily life. Discover the sacred dimension around you and consider ways in which you can serve the wider world (e.g. engagement in worthwhile causes for justice or the environment).

Fourth: While remaining open to other religious traditions, do decide on one specific spiritual path. We need to be fluent and at home in one religious expression rather than hopping from one to the other, picking up crumbs here and there. As a man who follows the path of Christ, I centre on this tradition and experience. This gives me a strong foundation for dialogue and a learning process with people from other backgrounds.

We are on the way, we are in evolution, and yet we are already there: we enter this world as spiritual beings and are here to unfold. This is one of the purposes of our incarnation. While many of us have lost sight of this larger context for our lives, at the core we are all already spiritual beings. I need to enter into the depth of my being in order to recognise my true identity as one of God's loved sons and daughters, a creation of His love. The point is to discover this identity and live out of this reality.

Therefore spirituality is no hobby, no Sunday pastime. It is not just one of many compartments in our lives. True spirituality permeates all spheres of human activity: sexuality, eating habits, political conduct, creativity, the use of money and so on. Spirituality is the point where we encounter our Higher Self, the reality of Christ in us. It encompasses and nourishes all aspects of our life.

I am aware that there are still Christians who have a problem with the term 'spirituality' and do not use it. In a conversation with the British gay Catholic theologian James Alison, he told me that he didn't like the word, which in his opinion invites a totally subjective religious experience. He feels that there is a danger of going from abusive dogmatism to the other extreme. So he prefers just to use the word 'faith' in all circumstances. My view is that, while the area of spirituality is open to abuse, as I have mentioned, nonetheless that experience of the spirit in our lives is essential and does not depend on church or dogma. 'The Spirit moves where he/she wills.' There is a certain surprise and newness to the experience. Later in this chapter I will add a criterion of discernment.

The concept of 'faith' also suffers a lot of abuse by many, from the religious right in the USA to the Opus Dei, who use it too. Another, more personal, reason why I like and use the word 'spirituality' has to do with my native language. In German we do not have different words for 'faith' and 'belief', only one: 'Glauben'. This word implies a strong belief in a religious dogma about God; it does not emphasise the element of faith and trust. For me, however, spirituality has to include trust. Faith is an experience, not a dogma.

Gay men, lesbian women and spirituality: where we are today

The current situation of gays and lesbians in relation to spirituality involves some major misunderstandings.

Like the population in general, many homosexual men and women do not make a distinction between spirituality and religion/church. While spirituality may be found within religion and the church, it is not the same thing. This causes much anger and confusion, since many queer men and women are fully aware of the harm that the major world religions (particularly Christianity and Islam) have done to gays and lesbians, and most queer people still regard homophobia and religion as inseparable.

When I started working for gays and lesbians in the spiritual context in 1979 and founded the nationwide Swiss gay and lesbian Christian organisation 'Homosexuelle und Kirche' (Homosexuals and the Church) three years later, I realised how much confusion there is. This was certainly not helped by the fact that often the most pious groups, with a fervent prayer life, were the most homophobic. So I experience a hesitation, even among those queer people interested in the Christian religious tradition, to explore and develop their spiritual life. While the homophobia of evangelical groups unfortunately continues and the press still has to report such disgraceful behaviour as the storm over the openly gay Anglican/Episcopal bishops, I have noted a change within the last quarter of a century. More and more gays and lesbians are aware that spirituality and homophobia do not necessarily come as a pair. It is also helpful that interest in a life-enhancing spirituality has increased. Many people are now realising that spirituality is something beyond sexual orientation and is the central dimension of life. This switch in consciousness has also slowly permeated the attitude of the gay and lesbian movement.

The same process has been taking place in my own life. My personal growth has been more nourished and encouraged by meditation, by what I have read about the experiences of Christian mystics and by transpersonal psychology (in my case Psychosynthesis) than by dogmatic statements from the church. The richness of new Christian literature, such as the books of Richard Rohr, has also given me much support. As far I can see, many people on a spiritual journey travel a similar path of growth. My personal experience has taught me how important it is to discover God not only as a partner in prayer but also as a reality in myself. Duality, the split of the material and spiritual, has found a healing corrective: Spirit encompasses the material but is still bigger than this, involving the mystery of incarnation of the divine and a personal relationship with a loving God.

It is not possible to 'nail down' God's spirit now and for ever. or to encapsulate it into a short message. While it is necessary to reflect on spirituality and to talk about it with others, you can only experience it with your heart and on your life journey. Theological and spiritual books are a big help but they do not replace the steps you take in your own life. It is the same with maps: You can study them over and over again. But they are not the town or the country itself. We have to choose to leave where we are and discover the new place ourselves.

This way into our own experience of God is exciting for gays and lesbians and allows us to become of age. In the reality of a liberating spirituality we are not dependent on the judgement of organised religion. Our power and our understanding come from another source. Whether we are engaged in traditional denominations or exploring new forms of church, we drink from our own well, from God in us.

Mutual influence – homosexuality and spirituality

At its deepest core, spirituality is beyond race, gender and sexual orientation. The now commonly used expression 'gay and lesbian spirituality', while obviously making a point and being well intended, has its limits. The reality of the divine, in whatever dimension we name it, is beyond and deeper than our sexual orientation. The cosmic dimension of God encompasses all of what we are personally and collectively and is not limited by it. Everybody who has been meditating or doing any serious spiritual exercise over many years will experience this reality sooner or later.

And yet our sexual orientation is important for our spiritual development and moulds our life journey. As I will point out in later chapters (like 'Homosexuality as Potential'), our being gay or lesbian is more then a genital expression and even goes beyond a love relationship. Being queer has also to do with our consciousness, which as a result may differ from that of the heterosexual majority.

Another effect on our spiritual life of being homosexual is our connection with the collective consciousness of gays and lesbian past and present. We cannot totally separate ourselves from the long history of homophobic oppression, violence and exclusion. In many places around the world this is still a sad reality. Many lesbians and gays are wounded because of this. Spirituality does not happen on some abstract level but works with the material that we are; and being gay or lesbian is part of what we are.

The opposite is also true: Our spirituality influences how we deal with our homosexuality. If I have the understanding that I am on a spiritual journey, then I will deal with my sex life in a holistic way. I will have respect for the dignity of my partner and myself. I will learn to understand my sexuality as a source of life energy.

As in the case of heterosexual couples, it makes a huge difference for same-sex couples if they choose to make spirituality a central focus of their life. The spiritual relationship, culture and pattern (e.g. prayer life) underpins their partnership and may be a source of creativity, fostering a will to work on faithfulness, mutual projects and difficult issues. (More about the meaning of spirituality in love relationships in Chapters 5 & 7)

Whoever lives with a spiritual awareness will become concerned about or even involved in issues relating to the future of this planet. True spirituality is never narcissistic but opens us up to caring for all that is around us.

From a confession of faith to an experience of God – the path of the mystic

All religions incorporate a mystical dimension: Judaism has the Kabbala, Islam the Sufi tradition. In the sixties many young women and men went to India, drawn by the mystic elements of Hinduism. Buddhism is spreading from Asia to parts of Europe and America and is welcomed by many for its strong emphasis on meditation as a mystic door. Traditional Christianity has rather oppressed its mystic dimension in the last few centuries but there is now an increasingly powerful resurgence of the Christian mystical tradition, especially since just after World War II.

Mysticism invites us to experience religion not with the head and a dogmatic viewpoint but with an emphasis on the heart and the deeper levels of consciousness. This does not mean that thinking and theology are totally unimportant; however, they are not the core of religion.

I myself grew up in a strictly religious and evangelical family and, by the time I was an adult, had received a huge dose of Bible teaching and Sunday school. At age 20 I attended an intensive 8-week Bible training and two years later I entered a theological seminary. Although this indulgence in theological thinking was certainly important, it was also a trap. All of this dogmatism and theology became a construct of thought and belief that took control of my life. I firmly believed in it all and yet I felt cut off from the stream of life. I was very aware that faith has an ethical dimension in life but most of what I was experiencing seemed moralising and artificial.

I use an image to illustrate this: In the Gospel there is the well-known story of the encounter of the Samaritan woman with Jesus at a well. She wants to give him water from the well. Jesus talks to her and opens her mind to the spiritual water of life. With this comparison the well becomes a symbol of the divine source of being. Many people in past and present times are in danger of debating the colour of the well, safety regulations, the age of the well, and its origin and history, while the real goal should be to get into the well itself and drink the water. A major part of the theology of all religions, especially in their fundamentalist and liberal extremes, is in danger of forgetting the well altogether. Going inside ourselves in meditation and prayer opens us to risk. We need to let go of the constructs of our thought. Only if we find the divine well can we formulate our faith and spiritual priorities. Then we shall express a spirituality which is authentic, courageous, refreshing and truthful.

Of course there are criteria for distinguishing real mysticism from the phoney kind or from spiritual claims that might even be dangerous. This is where our intellect comes into play. Gay contemporary mystic Andrew Harvey has, over and over again, emphasised that there are tests one can do. One important criterion is that true mysticism does not deny the dark side of human experience, including pain and mourning. David Steindl-Rast, the well known Californian monk and writer of Austrian origin, gives a list of points for use in discrimination, which I summarise:

• Mystic experience leads to justice and fair and loving action

• Mysticism engenders a great respect for the diversity of creation and the cosmic, all-encompassing dimension of the presence of God

• The mystic is full of awe and gratitude

• The mystic experience calls us to grow beyond a dualistic perception of the world; in Christian language, to discover the cosmic Christ in all things.

David Steindl-Rast did not write these criteria in a homosexual context, but his points make it obvious that a mystic journey and authentic spiritual experience automatically exclude such attitudes as homophobia.

Having had so much theological junk thrown at us, we queer men and women are especially fit and grace-filled to venture into a deep and honest spirituality. Let's stop engaging over and over again with the same people in endless discussions about those few phrases in the Bible that have been quoted out of context to exclude gay and lesbian people. At the time of working on the English version of this book, this abuse has been going on for about four decades. To return to our image of the well, instead of constantly biting into the stones, let's use our mouths to drink the water and to gain strength, power and love so that we can celebrate life.

Gays and lesbians in Christian mysticism and spirituality

I cherish great hopes that at least a major part of the worldwide Christian church will change and open up during the 21st century, growing from a confession of faith in a personal Christ to an experience of a cosmic Christ. As the aforementioned Catholic theologian Karl Rahner said, the Christian of the 21st century will be a mystic or he/she will not exist. Herein lies a special opportunity for gays and lesbians who are on a Christian spiritual journey. To experience God in the deep centre of the human heart – the main goal of the mystic path – opens up new perspectives and changes our awareness.

The common world-view still leans towards a dualistic perspective, even if the number of people with a sensibility for unity in diversity is growing. In the religious domain we see this dualistic view in all those fundamentalist distortions: in a banishment of God to the heavenly realm; in the perception of a God totally different from us, completely separated from creation. As I remember, my whole religious upbringing was very dualistic and, as a result, implicitly fostered a very negative view of humankind. There was the theory of the Holy Spirit who dwells in us (or at least in the Christian, as they said), but none of this talk was rooted in real experience, in our bodies and senses, and it was not at all liberating. While many groups from the so-called Pentecostal and charismatic churches gladly recognise a certain dimension of the Holy Spirit in humans who confess a faith in Christ, this aspect is often abused in order to put pressure on people and a moralistic judgementalism creeps in.

Even before I started my training and practice in Psychosynthesis I searched for role models who would teach me more than an intellectual or dogmatic approach to the reality of God. Along with all the valuable human role models, it was life itself that had the greatest impact in teaching me to find and open new doors. Experiences in meditation and getting to know the mystic tradition in depth were key parts of this journey

The Bible, particularly the New Testament, presents a mystical point of view. Just remember Jesus's parable of the vineyard: 'If you are in me and I am in you, you will bring forth much fruit' (John 15:5). Or take the dimension of the Cosmic Christ, who was there from the beginning of Creation and who encompasses everything: 'In Him (Christ) everything was created' (Col. 1:16).

The material world in its immense dimension is the body of God. Today's knowledge of the vast size of the universe fills me with awe and puts our world-view and image of God into perspective. Understanding the immensity of God changes our thinking and liberates us from narrow-minded images of the divine. We can only wonder at how many parochial people there are who still ignore the Cosmic Christ and prefer to worship a small, strict judge who controls human beings by peeking through keyholes. Away with it! God is expanding and is at the same time to be found in the smallest element. This feeling of being at home in the Spirit is what fulfils my deepest yearning.

A personal experience of queer Christian mysticism

My own personal openness to the mystical experience, to a spiritual depth of faith, gives me, over and over again, a sense of being at one with all life. When I am able to enter this deep level of myself, there is no exclusion, no cutting off. Many queer men and women have had experiences of being outcasts. I personally have experienced, and discovered in other people's lives, that such deep oneness in love can heal and empower us: in the end, Christ is in all there is: we are part of everything. This experience gives me the courage to deal openly with my fellow human beings and to engage in working for more justice for gays and lesbians. Additionally, this openness to the spiritual level gives me access to a non-dogmatic dimension of my Christian faith.

Feeling connected with and close to God allows me to find my centre and gives me strength and distance where necessary. I experience a balance in my identity. My homosexuality is part of what I am; my gayness is part of the divine reality. God is in me and in my body; my sexual expression has space in God. Everything is embraced by the Cosmic Christ.

I want to end this chapter with something I wrote after a time of meditation and personal prayer. Reflecting in prayer about the mystic dimension of being gay, I reached a very deep level and I listened to the voice of God from that space. I share these words as I received them and as I wrote them down: So the 'I' is the voice of Christ in me. Try to read this text with your heart rather than your head:

The mystic way is a way for gays and lesbians. Follow this way, all the way, now. Being lesbian, being gay, being one, being whole, being in Me as Christ, being new, being fearless, being in the centre, being in you, being in Me, being big and expansive, being strong in love.

In unity you will find diversity. In Me is everything, being gay and lesbian, everything is contained in me. I, Christ, was first before everything. The Word was there, the Word became flesh: the Word became bisexuality, heterosexuality, homosexuality; the Word became penis, testicles, vagina; every part of the body, sensitive for tenderness. The Word became fullness in diversity.

The more diversity, the more fullness. Only in the fullness of diversity do you see the image of the whole. The wholeness is the Omega, the goal of the road to unity. Homosexuality will help to connect men with men, women with women and women with men. This diversity is needed to make the richness of the human family visible. I am the centre, the Higher Self in the Cosmos. Who lives in me, lives in fullness in me, has eternal life.

QUESTIONS

What is your present stance concerning spirituality and being gay/lesbian?

Do you consider yourself as being on the Christian path? How does that relate to your sexuality?

In contrast to much of Eastern religion and a large part of so-called New Age spirituality, the Judaeo-Christian traditions hold the aspect of a personal God as very important – a loving 'Thou' or 'You' with whom you can enter a relationship in prayer, praise and thankfulness, but also with whom to wrestle. Jesus called God 'Abba' (a loving, close father or dad). Although less frequent, there are other titles, names and allusions to God as Friend, Lord, King, Lover, Eagle or Mother. In the Roman Catholic tradition Mary, the mother of Jesus, is also much honoured and provides a female dimension for many believers. How do you feel about those names and expressions of God? Which one do you feel most comfortable with? Are you in danger of reducing the personal aspect of God to an anthropomorphic concept (such as an old man with a beard in heaven or a strict judge)? Or are you more likely to consider God as merely an impersonal energy?

If you are not rooted in a Christian tradition, what are the names and orientation points on your spiritual path?

What do you associate with mysticism? Do you have any personal experience of it?

SUGGESTIONS

Take a large piece of paper and paint a river all the way from its source to the point where it flows into the sea or a lake. See the river as a symbol of your life. Draw or write along it the highlights of your spiritual development – for example your baptism, important experiences of God, involvement with a church, synagogue or temple – which have moulded you. Then write or draw symbols for important points along your journey as a gay man or a lesbian: your coming out process, your first sexual encounter and so on. Maybe there are other important aspects that you have discovered by reading this chapter. Meditate on what was and is important in your life journey and be alert for the connection between your sexuality and your spirituality. Get in touch with your desires for your present and future. Maybe you will want to put this drawing on the wall to help keep these thoughts in your awareness.

Read the account of Jesus at Jacob's well (John 4:1–26). Close your eyes and picture this story in its details. Imagine that you are meeting Jesus at this well. Get into a conversation with him. Ask for the water of life. Maybe you imagine yourself drinking from the well. Take time in your daily routine to recollect this image and to draw strength from it.

EXERCISE

Setting up and decorating a shrine or personal prayer corner

At the time of writing, my partner and I were in the privileged situation of living and working in a community house which had a spacious prayer and meditation room in the basement. Because of lack of space, many people may not be able to set aside an entire room for this purpose. Therefore look for a free corner or an unused wall in your home where you can build a shrine of your own which can serve as your place of prayer and meditation. On the floor, the wall or a low table, place objects that remind you of God's loving presence within you and in creation. These may be candles, icons, joss sticks, paintings of saints, pictures of spiritual teachers, precious stones, a prayer book, a Bible or other valued spiritual and religious books. Maybe you will also want to hang on the wall a sacred text or an important life-affirming statement.

Add to your shrine an object or a picture that represents your gay or lesbian nature. This may be a photo of your partner, of a lesbian theologian or of a gay mystic who is important to you. It may be a rainbow sign or a sensual homoerotic picture such as two men embracing or two women caressing each other tenderly.

Create your shrine with the clear intention that it will be a symbol of the divinity within you – for example, of your Christ-centredness. To be clear, it should be a representation and expression of God, not some kind of substitute or idol. In that way your shrine will also express your personal relationship with God. Or maybe you will want to demonstrate the cosmic dimension of Christ ('Everything has been created in him and through him'). If you are creative, you can bring together several aspects of God, but avoid overloading your place of prayer and therefore limiting or even trivialising your original intention with too many distractions.

Spend at least a short time each day in your personal prayer place. Whenever possible it would be ideal to do so for a while in the early morning and for a while in the evening or just before going to bed. If you have a partner or a lover, try to spend some time with him or her in this space of prayer and meditation. If you are part of a small group of spiritual seekers, meet around the shrine for worship or a meditation session. But in regard to other people who might not understand what this sacred space represents, don't be afraid to set boundaries to discourage them from trivialising, criticising or ridiculing this profound expression of your faith.

Among other things, use your shrine for:

- Silent meditation
- Personal prayer – conversations with God
- Visualisation exercises – to become aware of God's presence within
- Mantras
- Affirmations
- Singing and chanting
- Exercises involving the chakras or kundalini energy
- Consulting of wisdom cards
- Recitation of Bible verses
- Reading a chapter of a spiritual or theological book
- Reading a gay/lesbian book of daily inspirations, e.g. *The Word is Out* by Chris Glaser

PRAYER

Christ,
Help me to discover in myself the holy place,
just as I have created a sacred space in my home.
Guide me to return to this sacred spot
over and over again
and centre myself in your holy presence.
The Kingdom of God is within me.
Let me experience this treasure,
let it nourish me,
so that I might pass it on always anew.

Three

Homosexuality as Potential

In this chapter I explore the purpose and the potential of homosexuality. This approach is a central concern of my engagement in the gay and lesbian movement and one of the main intentions of this book. The time to debate how homosexuality developed is over. The question now is: What does it mean to be gay or lesbian, and what is its purpose? I am not the first gay person to move the goalposts and to ask about the potential and calling of being homosexual. In recent years this trend has become more prevalent in gay/lesbian spiritual literature, especially in the English-speaking world. It has in fact become a central focus of the spiritual gay and lesbian movement.

I begin with personal impressions from my own life experience and development. The challenging process of becoming conscious of my way of being in my early life recently prompted a profound reconsideration of the purpose and potential of being gay: I had always thought that my homosexuality first became apparent to me when I was about 13 years old, when I became aware of sexual impulses and romantic feelings towards the male sex. But a couple of years ago I realised that my being gay had expressed itself as far back in my childhood as I can remember. My earliest memories go back to November 1963, when I was less than four years old. Even then being gay affected me! Of course, not in the sense that I had sexual desires but in the sense that, despite being extremely young, I had a feeling of being unlike others, of having a different outlook towards the world around me.

Even at the age of six, when I entered kindergarten, I had a special sensibility and an acute sense of justice. I felt an intuitive connectedness with everything that was rare or threatened with extinction or exclusion This extended beyond children and adults to plants, animals and even cultural objects. My awareness and my senses were less attuned to what was considered normal or fashionable. I was interested in what was unusual and different – or queer, in the non-sexual sense of the word.

Over the following years of my childhood I found I had an unusual attitude towards gender roles and the two sexes. I realised that my perception of them was different from that of other boys. I had no urge to take on other boys in competitive games or fights or to share their mindset in any way. I was not interested in typically masculine sports. In contrast to most of my male peers at school and in my neighbourhood, I enjoyed playing with girls at least as much as with boys.

I remember well my dilemma at carnival time. My family, being pious, was generally biased against carnivals. Since the Basel Mardi Gras ('Fasnacht' in Swiss German) has such a high profile during its three-day festivities, it was impossible even for my parents to totally ignore or deny it. This carnival was, and still is, such an integral part of the local culture. Thinking about this Mardi Gras kept me busy every year in February or March as the festival drew closer. The traditional wearing of masks was strictly forbidden by my parents but they did tolerate my wearing a costume. On one occasion I took my father's old baker's uniform and walked around all in white wearing the conspicuous baker's hat. Another year I dressed myself up as a cowboy. I think I was six years old when I got the idea of dressing myself as an 'Old Aunt'. An 'Old Aunt' (Alti Tante in Swiss German) is traditional female attire for men at the carnival; a kind of middle-aged or older lady dolled up in bright colours. The fact that I wanted to dress that way as a young boy was quite extraordinary. My parents and grandmother had very mixed feelings but they gave the green light as long as I did not wear a mask. So I got myself all dressed up and even put on some lipstick and other make-up. Some people were a bit astonished but all went well.

As I was thinking and dreaming about my costume the following year, I found myself wondering if it would be possible to connect or mix the two polarities of male and female. How about a male aunt or a female cowboy?! My head and heart were busy but I could not find a solution that satisfied me. This whole process and inner conflict was a growthful step towards a higher sensibility and an integration of 'female' and 'male' within myself. Needless to say, I went through all this without any hint of support from my school, friends or family.

Of course, I am aware that not every gay man has been through exactly the same process during his childhood. However, since 1978 I have met hundreds of gays and lesbians at conferences, in counselling situations and privately. From talking with them and also from reading many books on the subject, I have become convinced that my personal experience as a child has many parallels in the lives of the vast majority of gays and lesbians.

The lesbian American theologian Melanie Morrison describes her own awareness of being different as she grew up in her book *The Grace of Coming Home.* She felt her 'otherness' as a very young girl, before sexuality and intimate relationships could be an issue:

> *From a very early age, I felt at home in overalls and jeans and experienced distress whenever I wore a dress. Unlike my sisters, I was not particularly attracted to dolls or tea parties or other indoor games. Every chance I got, I would be outdoors, fantasising that my bicycle was a powerful motorcycle or that I was winning a marathon bicycle race. I was playing every sport imaginable – baseball, football, basketball, ice hockey, tennis. [...] Throughout grade school, I played sports in school and in the neighbourhood. I was captain of the Marble Elementary School football team – the only girl on an all-male team. There were some good things about this cross-gender behaviour: I felt pride in being different from the other girls; up to a certain age, the boys were admiring of my athletic skills; my parents were supportive of my unorthodox dress and activities.*

The Grace of Coming Home (pp.49/50)

Later in her book she recounts vividly how it was precisely this transgressing of the orthodox gender rules that opened up her consciousness. As an openly lesbian minister she still draws strength from this expanded awareness.

Let's take a look at this issue from another angle. Historically, among many indigenous groups homosexual people took on special functions. For example, a number tribes in North America used the term 'Bedaches' for homosexually inclined men. These 'Bedaches' assumed the role of healers. Our own culture, too, would be far poorer if it lacked the same-sex contribution or had never had homosexually oriented artists like Michelangelo. In the last couple of centuries the proportion of homosexual or bisexual men and women active in the arts, in social ministry, in social reform movements and in the clerical professions has consistently been higher than among the general population. So it was no surprise, for example, that when the first wave of AIDS hit the population of New York in the 1980s, the large and important theatre community suffered greatly from the death of many of its gay contributors.

As early as 1914, in an act of true pioneer spirit, Edward Carpenter made an important and challenging observation. In his book *Intermediate Types Among Primitive Folk* he presented and commented on the special duties that gay men (and to a lesser extent lesbian women) were called to perform in the ancient world. As mentioned above, this was noticeable particularly amongst indigenous peoples such as those of North America. Carpenter used a scientific approach to substantiate his hypotheses and provided comprehensive examples. His discoveries and conclusions are fascinating. He listed the roles of homosexually inclined people among these populations as fourfold:

- As prophets or priests
- As wizards or witches
- As inventors of the arts and the crafts
- As hermaphrodites among gods and mortals

Carpenter noticed that gay and lesbian people were often recognised as such even in childhood, when the parents or other people of the tribe sensed the 'differentness' of the child. In those cultures, this was a reason to rejoice! The males who were discovered to be different had to wear the attire of the other sex, and sometimes even a third gender was invented. Naturally we cannot go back in time and we cannot blindly copy things from the past. To put it concisely: evolution goes forward not backward. But the underlying pattern, intention and vision I do consider to be timeless. It up to us to rediscover it and to translate it for our present time; and to live our truth in our own cultural context and state of consciousness.

Of course, some of the greater sensibility of past and present generations of gays and lesbians stems from the fact that the oppression many of them have experienced may have made them more sensitive and fostered their feeling of solidarity with other outcasts. In addition, being an outsider opens up your horizons and allows you a different perspective on your culture. This obviously fosters artistic creativity. But I am convinced that this is only part of the reason for the differences in consciousness and awareness among gays and lesbians. In a growing number of countries oppression of homosexuals is now much reduced, and in a few instances has disappeared altogether, but the gift of difference in sensibility remains. Many people, including myself, experienced a different kind of awareness even before explicitly recognising their homosexuality and before experiencing any possible oppression or discrimination.

Important in this context is my conviction that there are three (interconnected) levels of (homo-) sexuality. In addition to the level of genital-sexual expression and the level of love relationships, there is a third level in the area of personal consciousness. I will explore these three dimensions further in the chapter 'Sexuality as a source of strength'.

David Philbedge, a gay Buddhist living in England, tells of his memories from his own youth:

I'd felt from a very early age an outsider, which I think is a common experience for gay men – as you grow up you feel somewhat out of synch from the other people around you. It shifted my perspective, my attitude to life in general, which basically manifested itself in me being incredibly discontented and difficult. If you have a sense that you are different from what's around you, you're not going to get sucked in without thinking, you're not going to accept received wisdom. All worthwhile spiritual paths involve asking questions: it's that sense of being an outsider that maybe begins that process. Spirituality is about realising your place in the world: if you're lesbian and gay, your position in the world is going to be different from what other people tell you, and from their position in the world.

From Queer to Eternity, p.28

The renowned theologian and proponent of creation spirituality Matthew Fox wrote a chapter called 'The Spiritual Journey of the Homosexual' in the book *A Challenge to Love in the Church – Gay and Lesbian Catholics*. In this chapter he states that a few years previously he was working on a retreat together with Sister José Hobday, a Franciscan nun of Native American origin. He remembers:

One day she took me aside with great seriousness and said she had a question she had to put to me as a representative of white society. 'I cannot understand,' she began, 'the hang-up in white culture and Church towards the homosexual. In our native tradition we don't even have a word for homosexual. And it is well known among us that often the homosexual was the most spiritual member of a tribe, who played powerful roles as counsellors to some of our most important chiefs.' She went on to explain how in her ministry of retreat-giving, the people she encountered who were 'the most beautiful Christians of all' were very often homosexual men and women. This had been my experience as well.

p.189

There is a double tragedy underlying the widespread homophobia of Christianity and of the other traditional world religions with patriarchal tendencies. Firstly because of the immense suffering it has caused to gays and lesbians. Secondly because the church and other religious institutions have lost so much in the area of creativity, healing, service and joy through the oppression or exclusion of homosexual men and women.

To repeat my earlier point, enough time has been spent in puzzling over how the same-sex orientation came into being or developed. It is now crucial to explore and visualise the purpose for which homosexuality exists, the contribution it can make to a more human world, and how gays and lesbians can integrate and live their sexuality in realisation of the power of God that permeates everything.

I firmly believe that homosexuality is as important as heterosexuality for the evolution of humanity. To put it more controversially and extremely, although heterosexuality is naturally of the highest importance for ensuring reproduction and hence the physical evolution of the human species, homosexuality is a vital driving force in the spiritual evolution of human consciousness.

The evolution of human consciousness is ongoing. This view is expounded by the leading explorers of this process in the last hundred years: Sri Aurobindo, Jean Gebser, Pierre Teilhard de Chardin and today's Ken Wilber and Andrew Cohen. Their basic conviction is that the human family, having travelled through the magic, then mythic, then mental consciousness levels, is now in the process of entering a new arena of consciousness. The term most often used for this new stage is 'integral consciousness'. In a Christian context this model can help us to read the numerous passages in the Bible about the end of the world, the New Jerusalem, the Second Coming of Christ, with a much more profound understanding and in a way that is accessible to men and women of the 21st century. Often these texts have caused people to fear the future and to be passive in face of it. The evolutionary approach encourages us to be active and open to a process of transformation. As a result, it is possible to comprehend these texts in a new way, with a sense of liberation.

With a prophetic voice, the writer and former Catholic monk Toby Johnson explains evolution in the context of the modern gay and lesbian movement:

In the big picture, it seems, a new sexual identity has developed among human beings in the last hundred years. [...]
This is something new. It's like the human species is evolv-

ing a new sex. Isn't this a potentially momentous event in human evolution? Shouldn't this phenomenon be of major interest to anthropologists and sociologists and futurists and philosophers of all sorts? If human beings were beginning to develop a new organ in their bodies, wouldn't everybody be interested in learning what it is and what it is for, not trying to deny it and wishing it would go away? Well, in homosexuals, the planet is growing a new kind of human being, a new organ of the collective. Everybody should be interested and supportive. This is what the lesbian and gay rights movement is really about.

ReCreations, p.85

We can see the whole movement in a much larger context. The integration of homosexuality is as important a step in the growth of humanity as the widespread abolition of slavery, racist structures, and the battle for the equality of women. In that sense the integration of homosexuality is vital to a wider and more mature human consciousness. It has to come about as part of the ongoing unfoldment of creation.

The overall goal is unity in diversity. We are experiencing a transition from mental consciousness to integrative consciousness. This process has its painful aspects and phases of chaos and disorientation, which is what we are experiencing at present; but the changes are necessary. After separation must come integration if we are to survive.

I have a dream, I have a vision

I see the human family thankfully embracing its gay and lesbian siblings.

I see queers and straights hand in hand, learning from their own different gifts.

I see gays and lesbians as healers, liturgists, dancers, deacons, priests, researchers, explorers, reformers.

I see lesbians and gays at the forefront of spiritual development and as pathfinders for a new consciousness.

QUESTIONS

Try to remember: How did you experience yourself as different when you were a child, when you were an adolescent and in later years?

Look at being gay or lesbian, at your sexuality, in the light of this chapter. What were your particular signs and manifestations of being different? To what extent did you experience another kind of awareness or altered perception?

SUGGESTIONS

Reflect on the word 'potential'. Brainstorm what it means for you and write it down.

Become aware that homosexuality is a gift for humanity and that it has a deep meaning. Link mentally with the countless homosexual and bisexual men and women in the past and in the present who have lived or live their potential to the full.

Dream and visualise in your mind how lesbians and gays can contribute during the next years or decades to overcoming the life-threatening ecological crisis faced by humanity and the planet. How can we find for ourselves a healing and creative place in the world community?

EXERCISE

Psychosynthesis inner dialogue exercise

Sit in a comfortable upright position or lie on the floor. Close your eyes and become aware of your breathing for a moment.

Now imagine that you are in a valley full of flowers on a warm and sunny morning. You are in a wonderful place. Gradually become aware of your environment: the valley with the flowers, the intensely blue sky, the clean air, and the morning breeze gently caressing your cheeks. Feel the contact of your feet with the ground and be aware of what clothing you are wearing.

You feel a sense of readiness and expectancy. As you look around, you see a mountain. It towers above you and looking at its summit gives you a sense of excitement.

You notice a path leading towards the mountain. You decide to follow it. The path takes you into a forest. You can smell the pleasant aroma of the pine trees and sense the cool, dark atmosphere.

Now you see the path leading out of the forest and becoming steeper. Walking uphill, you can feel the muscular effort demanded of your body and the energy that pleasantly suffuses it. The path becomes steeper and steeper; perhaps you have to use your hands to help yourself climb.

The air is getting fresher. You have a sense of exhilaration and notice the silence of the surroundings. Your climb takes you into a cloud. Everything is whitish and misty. You proceed carefully and cautiously. Now the cloud dissolves and you can see the sunny sky again above you.

Up here, everything is much brighter and clearer. The air is clean, the colours round about you are vivid, and the sun is shining. Climbing is easier now. You seem to weigh less, and you feel drawn to the summit and are eager to reach it.

You are now on top of the mountain, on a plateau. Far off, you see someone. It is a wise and loving person. You feel his/her readiness to listen to what you have to say and to answer your questions. He/she has noticed you. You are walking towards each other. More and more, you feel the presence of this wise person. It is an emanation of joy, holiness, power and love.

Now you are facing each other. You have the chance to ask questions of this wise and loving person and to share your concerns. Ask him/her the following questions and allow yourself some time before becoming aware of each answer:

- Where does the potential of homosexuality lie?
- What gifts and talents are trying to emerge in my life?
- What one concrete step can I take in my life that will allow me to live my potential more fully?

Possibly the answers will come in words, but pay attention to any symbols or gestures. Whatever the answer is, do not judge or dismiss it. You may want to ask more questions or perhaps prolong the dialogue. Whatever happens, notice the answers.

Show gratitude, in whatever form you prefer, and say goodbye to this wise person, knowing that you can come back at any time to the top of this mountain.

Now, at your own speed and in your own time, walk all the way back down the mountain until you get to the valley full of flowers, the place where you started your journey. Then slowly open your eyes, get up, stretch, drink something and write down notes on this inner journey, with particular attention to the answers you received.

(The above guided visualisation is based on an exercise devised by Roberto Assagioli, the founder of Psychosynthesis, and further developed by Piero Ferrucci in his highly recommended book What We May Be, *on which my version is based.)*

PRAYER

Christ,
As a plant develops from a seed,
let me become what I am.
Help me to discover my potential,
to recognise the opportunities offered me
by being gay (or lesbian),
and to live my talents.
Give me the courage to be moved by my dreams
and to act on them.
May my personal transformation contribute
to the evolution of humanity's consciousness.
Empower me to great actions through your spirit.

Four

Being Gay or Lesbian – Gifts and Opportunities

After some basic reflections on potential in the last chapter I want to focus attention on specific practical gifts, talents, callings, opportunities and, ultimately, responsibilities that might result from a homosexual orientation. I invite you on a journey of discovery as I outline the nature of these gifts. For some of you this might be new territory, while for others it may be a homecoming.

In the Bible we find passages where people's special abilities are emphasised: 'Each one of you has been given a special gift.' John McNeill, in *Taking a Chance on God* (p.93/94), goes along with the approach of many liberation theologies in saying that various groups of people are given specific gifts. In this sense I agree with McNeill that homosexuality too incorporates certain capacities. He understands these to be most commonly the gifts of compassion, hospitality and the joy of play.

What follows is a practical list of specific gifts, callings and responsibilities that are within the potential of gays and lesbians. Some might call them queer gifts. I give a short introduction to each of them. I came up with this list partly from my own life experience and partly from some of the best of gay spiritual literature, to the authors of which I am thankful for the inspiration I have received: Chris Glaser, John McNeill, Elisabeth Stuart and many others.

I am not saying that every homo- or bisexual person must have all the talents described below. This list is to be understood as a tool and inspiration for personal searching and inquiry. It is my hope that readers will discover or learn more about their own particular calling and gifts.

When I made a list of all possible queer talents and gifts I discovered 28 different ones! For this book I have selected fourteen.

1. Spiritual and religious openness

According to C.G. Jung, homosexual people are especially open to religious feelings but, of course, that has caused a lot of suffering because of the homophobic traditions of most world religions, which could not appreciate that openness. I myself felt very religious from an early age. In my 25-year-long engagement in working for gays and lesbians I have discovered that many people have that same lifelong openness to the divine presence. Lesbians and gays have always been people with an extraordinary religious receptivity. During his many years as a psychotherapist C.G. Jung observed in the spiritual life of his homosexual clients what he called 'a richness of religious feeling, which brings to life an "Ecclesia Spiritualis" and a spiritual receptivity that is an open door to divine revelation'. (C.G. Jung here and below quoted after Hopcke & Thompson). This is a further explanation as to why so many people in spiritual occupations are gay or lesbian.

2. Sensibility

Sensibility is an important prerequisite for discerning what reforms are needed in society and also for being artistically creative. Sensibility includes delicacy and having a 'radar' for the extraordinary.

C.G. Jung hints at another uniqueness in the inner life of gay and lesbian people which could be a huge gift for humanity in this violent and materialistic age: the capacity to develop friendships. Unfortunately he speaks only of men and leaves lesbians out of the picture, due either to his own reservation or his use of language. Nevertheless Jung says that 'homosexual people have a differentiated Eros. This gives homosexuals a greater capacity for friendship, which often leads to connections of astonishing tenderness between men and may even enhance the friendship between the sexes. They may also have a good and aesthetic taste, which is fostered through the presence of the feminine aspect.'

Women are often regarded as sensitive in a problematic sense – as being weak and not able to take on tough responsibilities. Lesbians will need to discover for themselves – and are already doing so – what true sensibility means for them.

3. Improved same-sex interaction

A further potential of homosexuality lies in the fact that humanity urgently needs an improvement in male-to-male and female-to-female relationships.

It is obvious to many that the sexes need to complement each other. But sometimes this is emphasised in a one-sided, heterosexual way and the concept is abused to classify gays and lesbians as pathological. But what is often overlooked is that gays and lesbians already engage with each other in friendship and are therefore able to complement the other sex. Moreover, we all carry the polarities of 'female' and 'male' within ourselves, whatever our sexual orientation, so we are able – and I would say called – to reconcile and integrate these opposites within our own selves.

But to return to my main point: the importance of people of the same sex being able to interact in a complementary manner cannot be over-emphasised. It is lacking in men more than in women. Most violence happens between men. It is usually men who plan wars and armies still consist mostly of men. So it's men fighting men. The competitive mentality is still strong.

Therefore same-sex sexuality is a significant part of the spectrum of the urgently needed ability of people of the same sex to complement each other. Lesbian and gay couples show clearly and explicitly that same-sex understanding is possible and can be lived. Seeing such examples may encourage closeness, friendship, touching and a general coming together of people of the same sex in daily life. When someone no longer condemns homosexuality, it is easier for them to express tenderness in their contact with members of the same sex.

4. Alternative gender roles

Above all, in general gay and lesbian people are in less danger of projecting the characteristics of the opposite sex (for lesbians the masculine, for gays the feminine) outside of themselves, and of seeing them as embodied only in the other sex. They are much more able to discover the opposite aspect within themselves and integrate it within their whole being.

Lesbians and gays can help to change the clichés about gender roles and the fixed expectations of the different sexes. This process is very obviously already taking place. On a trivial level, for example, it can be seen in the generally stronger fashion sense of men nowadays or even in something like their opennness to wearing earrings, which might not have come about if gay men had not led the way. More important, perhaps, are the changes in expectation concerning gender roles within relationships: Same sex relationships can show the world how to live in a creative partnership with another person without fixed role expectations. This could lead to a major shift of much more significance than an interest in fashion, in that it might inspire a redefinition of the content and quality of marriage.

As Andrew Harvey has pointed out, queer people have a unique function in that they see the craziness and cruelty of the patriarchal society and can help others to transcend it. He describes this from a gay male perspective when he goes on to say:

> *We've had a false masculine presented to us, an ideal of control and domination that is really a frozen hysteria, a condensation of panic and fear. It has nothing to do with the real masculine. In fact, gay men are closer to the real masculine then the so-called masculine ones are. Gay men in the way in which they interpret and live masculinity might be models for straight men, models for a deepening of the heart, a more tender and playful humour, a greater acceptance and tolerance and diversity.*

(Gay Soul, p.62)

5. Sense of justice

As I mentioned before, when I was a child I was aware of a simple and deep-rooted sense of justice in myself, an intuitive connection with children, adults and even animals, plants and cultural aspects that were rare or in a minority, that were in danger of extinction or were threatened or banished. Many lesbians and gays experience similar feelings before they become fully aware that they themselves are in a minority. The later recognition, as adults, that they belong to a group that is in many ways discriminated against or violated builds on and strengthens their intuitive sense of justice and compassion. It also leads to a sense of solidarity with all other gays and lesbians and beyond that with various other oppressed groups.

6. Healers and shamans

Many ancient cultures acknowledge a connection between homosexuality and shamanism. I have already mentioned the so-called Bedaches of Native North American tribes. These were men who took on a healing ministry and who had a different gender understanding in the sense that they dressed differently and, as far as we know, often embodied a homosexual orientation and lifestyle. Today there are gay and lesbian Native Americans who are researching this tradition; much of it was destroyed by the settlers from Europe as part of their general violence toward the native population.

In North America today (and slowly in other parts of the world) there are groups that call themselves Radical Faeries who work on developing healing rituals. The work of Andrew Ramer and his Body Electric School – mainly the fostering of body and sexual awareness and healing potential in gay men – is also becoming more widespread. Lesbian women are often very active within the women's movement, working to discover their healing powers and a few even going so far as trying to reinvent the concept of 'witchcraft' in a positive manner. For many these movements seem to be too extreme in their beliefs and practices and one may question if some are indeed in danger of falling into the prepersonal/transpersonal fallacy – mistaking a prepersonal experience for a transpersonal state. But we have to recognise that these movements ask important questions and open up the vision of gays and lesbians as healers.

7. Hospitality

The story of the destruction of Sodom and Gomorrah has been constantly misused in recent centuries to prove the so-called sinfulness of homosexuality. But not only has that misinterpretation had dire consequences for lesbians and gays, it has also encouraged the committing of the very 'sin' that is central to that biblical story – that of being inhospitable to others. How many people have been thrown out of their churches, synagogues and mosques and denied a welcome because of this misguided interpretation!

The very fact that most gays and lesbians never start a traditional family could mean that they have the gift of living hospitality in a special way. This has been very important in my own life with my partner Emanuel in living in serving communities, where we accepted people from difficult life situations. As gay and lesbian people, we are able to explore new forms of family. Hospitality can be expressed in many different ways and this is certainly a quality which we desperately need in our often individualistic and anonymous society.

8. Consciousness scouts/agents of change

According to Andrew Ramer (*Gay Soul*, p.71,73) gays and lesbians can be 'consciousness scouts' and 'agents of change'. Two factors inspire us to this prophetic calling:

Our greater openness to both polarities, male and female, within ourselves allows us to access more areas of our consciousness. Outsiders ask questions. People on the edge often ask different questions from the ones that insiders ask; also they challenge the familiar. They look at the world differently and may have a queer insight.

Coming out raises the awareness. The process of coming out has consequences for our consciousness. We take an intense, critical and positive look at our sexuality, and we let go of any expectation of being accepted and respected in all of society. We open ourselves to the risk of being discriminated against or misunderstood. Out of that evolves an examination of oneself and the world that many heterosexuals don't experience. We learn to be truly honest and develop what Peter Sweasey (in *From Queer to Eternity*) calls a 'bullshit detector', an instinctive ability to recognise lies and all that is phoney, superficial and shallow.

Since lesbians and gays usually do not procreate, they are rather more open than others to change and risk in their lives and the courage it takes to face that.

All these experiences encourage lesbians and gays to take on a strong leadership role in the process of change in the world, which is what, among other things, we need in these dangerous and challenging times. It will be interesting to see to what extent we, as gay and lesbian people, develop in that direction. The need for a greater acceptance of homosexuality worldwide seems to grow in parallel with the absolute necessity for a quantum leap in the evolution of human consciousness (from mental to integral consciousness).

The queer (in more than one way) author, socialist and philosopher Edward Carpenter, writing at the beginning of the 20th century, expressed his often controversial views in his books. For example, he wrote of his vision: ' ... that the homosexual people may be destined to form the advance guard of that great movement which will one day transform the common life by substituting the bond of personal affection and compassion for the monetary, legal and other external ties which now control and confine society.' (*The Intermediate Sex*, Ch. 5, Internet version)

9. Artist, creator of beauty

Gay Jungian Robert Hopcke says: 'We see things differently, that is the purpose of art.' (*Gay Soul*, p.219)

In spite of their minority status homosexual and bisexually inclined people have achieved exceptional and outstanding things in the area of art throughout the centuries – from Michelangelo to Noel Coward, from Rita Mae Brown to Virginia Woolf. I think that our mode of existence encourages our artistic creativity to develop beyond the norm. We stand outside of the consensus of normality. This inspires us to new creations, beyond what is customary. It makes one wonder how much the churches, too, could learn, if they were open to everyone without restriction.

You cannot exclude homosexuality without also excluding art.

10. Called to mysticism

As discussed previously (see Chapter 2) gays and lesbians have a special opportunity to experience the mystic dimension of faith. Andrew Harvey, perhaps the greatest living gay mystic, argues (and I think we can include lesbians too in his conclusions):

If only gay men [and lesbians] understood that mystics have shared throughout history so much of the same derision and persecution as they have, for some of the same reasons, because what they incarnated was the banished feminine, the derided powers of intuition, the powers of sacred love and sacred joy. If gay men [and lesbians] could be guided to understand their own sensitivity and yearning for the love as coming from within their innermost core, which is a divine source, then you could really see a spiritual revolution among them' [...]

That's why gay [and lesbian] mystics are so important: they show gay men [and lesbian women] that there is a way to enter into direct communication with the divine source and its unconditional transforming love that bypasses all dogma and punitive moralism.

Gay Soul, p.61

11. Reconciliation of sexuality and spirituality

A great service we can offer to humanity, and also to its religious traditions, is that of bringing together sexuality and spirituality. Many of us have grown up with the message that a sexual life and a faith journey do not belong together, that our sexuality does not please God. As gays and lesbians we have gone through a process of reconciling spirituality and sexuality and as a result have become more mature. The next step is perhaps the question of how sexuality and spirituality can actively enrich each other. More about this in the chapter 'Sexuality as a source of strength'.

I believe that through wrestling with spirituality and sexuality, we contribute to bringing these forces together to create a new energy in their synthesis. All churches and all people who are sufficiently open can learn from this process.

12. Inner authority

In *From Queer to Eternity* the author makes the point that one of the main spiritual gifts of 'being queer' is the freedom from rigid social and religious norms. This can lead to our discovering, strengthening and trusting our own inner authority.

With this perspective we are called to follow in the footsteps of Jesus, who lived by his own inner authority. Whenever I read about fundamentalist tendencies in contemporary religions and get sad, afraid or angry, it is helpful for me to go to our sanctuary and pray in front of the icon of Christ. Sometimes I express my pain and my anger out loud. But always I hear a voice in me saying: 'I had the same experience. I was crucified by the fundamentalists of my time. I understand your frustration and your anger. I am with you; I am in you on your journey. Have courage to go on your way and trust in life.'

If we walk with our heads up and are open about our faith and our being queer, then we grow into an inner authority. This authority in the depth of our being can be a healthy challenge to those around us, and may further widen not only our own horizons but also those of our neighbours.

13. Teaching and mentoring

Clearly, this is not the appropriate place to discuss the artificial insemination of lesbians or the adoption rights of gay couples. What I want to mention is a totally different possibility for engaging with children and young people. I feel that gays and lesbians could play a vital role as a new kind of godfather or godmother – a mentor to nourish boys and girls on their journey to adulthood. I know of a gay man who has made a commitment to guide fatherless boys into adulthood. He does so by joining in their leisure time, listening to them wholeheartedly and being a shining example. Recently I read about a group of gay men in the USA who formed a connection with a kindergarten and a school in a poor area and contributed to the quality of the children's life by organising parties, giving them useful gifts and just being present with the children.

Of course, a certain amount of prejudice remains in society and there are still people who will assume that gay men in particular are more likely to be paedophiles. But such prejudice will gradually disappear. A whole new challenge for lesbians and even more so for gay men could grow out of the area of mentoring. This is because a significant proportion of children (different from country to country) grow up lacking the presence of a strong father figure. Boys in particular could profit from a male mentor who guides them as they grow into manhood and helps them find creative ways of being a man.

Even C.G. Jung addresses the issue, although again unfortunately he mentions only men: 'The homosexual may be excellently gifted as a teacher because of his nearly female inward view and tactfulness.' The word 'female' may not represent the best choice of term. Gay and lesbian pedagogy has more to do with the gift of intuition and the capacity to guide without manipulation. In practical terms that means the ability to sense in which direction young people want to grow, to let the individual discover this and to foster him or her without reservation.

14. New ways of being prolific

We are called to conceive 'spiritual children'. Over-population and high birth rates are still a big problem in many parts of the world, in addition to our abuse of the planet's resources. During my own lifetime the number of people on Earth has more or less doubled! Further billions are likely to be added during the 21st century. Obviously there are already enough people on this planet. We don't need greater numbers but rather a quality of life. Gays and lesbians – especially as same-sex couples – demonstrate how sexuality and partnership can be lived creatively without the need to birth children. They embody a different way of being prolific.

From this point of view it is important that homosexual relationships are lived and recognised globally as an alternative lifestyle – not just in Europe, America and a few other countries but worldwide from Algeria to Zimbabwe .

Andrew Harvey makes a strong point about this:

> *Gay men and women would clearly be seen for what they are from birth – as beings essential to the health of society; as people who are freed from the responsibilities of procreation to cultivate the artistic, the spiritual, the values of living itself, as people who point to an inner fusion of male and female, a holy androgyny, that all beings could aspire to.*

(Gay Soul, p.56)

Any of the gifts mentioned above can be a sign of the new way of being prolific. Everybody can ask himself or herself what specific 'spiritual child' he or she wants to 'birth' in this world. Anyone can become 'pregnant' and 'fertile' in the many dimensions of this new life.

QUESTIONS

How do you feel when you hear about the gifts and opportunities of being gay/lesbian?

Are there any people in your life with whom you can enter into a constructive exchange of ideas about your possible talents? If not, how could you get in contact with men and women like that?

What have you done in your life to discover and test your giftedness and to apply your talents to the reality of life?

SUGGESTIONS

Repeat over and over the following phrase: 'If I had enough courage I would … ' and finish this phrase by naming activities or life decisions. Make a list and see if there are things on it which you actually might be able to do!

Along with all these considerations about your life, also take a look at your current work situation. Can you use your gifts in that setting? Or do you use your talents in your spare time? Does a change of job or profession seem an option that would help you to live more fully?

Read further books that encourage you to live your talents and take the opportunities that life offers you. (See bibliography)

EXCERCISE

Dance ritual: Queer talents and gifts

Place a large, thick candle in a fireproof holder in the middle of the room. Instead of a burning candle you could use an icon, a crucifix, incense sticks or something that positively represents God or the transpersonal for you. Also take a piece of paper and write on it in large, visible letters 'Homosexuality as potential'. Place this piece of paper next to the candle or whatever symbol you have chosen.

Now take a further 14 sheets of paper and write very visibly on them the 14 different gifts which are specifically mentioned in this chapter

– one gift to one piece of paper. Arrange these sheets of paper around the main one (Homosexuality as potential) and the symbol.

Now go to your CD or cassette collection and choose a few pieces of music that make you feel comfortable and that inspire you to dance and move freely. You may like world music such as African dance or Indian chants; or maybe you prefer a melodious classical track or a joyful rock song or an uplifting jazz piece or toe-tapping show music. If you have chosen a song, take care that the lyrics do not distract you.

While you let the music play, let yourself go, and move and dance freely around the symbols and the sheets of paper in the centre of your room. Merge into the music; let the melody or the rhythm move you. Experience your body and your senses; enjoy the dancing.

After warming up for a while, notice more and more the sheets of paper with the 14 different suggested gifts and callings. Now listen to your intuition to see which one of the sheets (and therefore talents) you are most attracted to at this moment.

After 10 minutes, or whatever time you need, stop the music and meditate on the chosen gift. Ask yourself if and how you already live it. What do you need in order to translate this talent into your daily life? Let spontaneous prayers and visions emerge from within you. Maybe a symbol will appear in your mind which you would like to draw.

What step could you take next in your life in order to make this talent a reality? Maybe you have to make a decision now, or at some later date.

PRAYER

God,
Thank you for the many facets of my lesbian or gay nature.
I am amazed at my potential
and the gifts and opportunities that flow from it.
I also praise you for the talents of my lesbian sisters
and gay brothers.
Help me, help us, to use these talents and our ability
to be prolific for the welfare of all of us,
the human family and the whole of creation.
Help us,
that the heightening of our awareness as lesbians and gays,
may contribute to the urgently needed evolution
of humankind's consciousness.

Five

Partnership of Love

Why does the idea of same-sex partnerships and, even more so, gay marriage make so many people splutter with rage? What crucial button does it push in the human psyche?

In the last chapter I touched on the potential for same-sex relationships to enrich the life of the world. (In the following chapter on sexuality there is also the testimony of a lesbian who sees her partnerless state as a gift and a further exploration of the power of sexuality.) How can a same-sex partnership embody and express the love of God?

I want to start with my own and my partner Emanuel's situation. The order to which we belong accepts people not only as individual men and women but also in terms of their relationships with others, whether they are single and celibate, or heterosexually married or in a same-sex partnership. Our status as same-sex partners in a 'life partnership' is recognised. The latter is described as follows:

> *By life partnership we mean two persons of the same sex who have decided to enter a committed relationship and have asked for God's blessing. The acceptance of this way of life into the structures of the order is an important part of our calling. In a world which is in danger of disintegrating because of the social or economic alienation of different groups of people, it is the reconciling, integrating and healing power of love that reflects the message of living as an organism in Christ. That is why differences between humans, in this case based on sexuality, should not lead to separation and disassociation but to a wholeness and mutual enrichment. Given this status, homosexual people who have no calling to a celibate life have the opportunity to take a vow to a committed partnership and can therefore live with their partner according to their wish in full engagement with the order and in a radical emulation of Christ.*
>
> *Because a same-sex couple cannot give birth to physical children, the power of being together in availability for God*

and for those around them expresses itself rather in the potential and work of parenting 'spiritual children' and in being fruitful/productive in doing the work of God in this world. On a practical level this can mean the couple offers hospitality with warmth and acceptance, and this may also include people in need or isolation. Because gay and lesbian people have experienced being outsiders and mavericks in society, they are called to show a special compassion to other outcasts. As sexually different people they are acutely affected by the 'Christian' sexual morality that, even to this day, associates sexuality with dirt, sin and base urges. This in turn is matched by the 'worldly' tendency to see sexuality as an arena of consumerism and ego-gratification.

Homosexual as well as heterosexual Christians have a duty to work to counteract these misunderstandings – to make sure that sexuality is acknowledged and lived again as a holy force, as a language of love, as an experience of the divine in ecstasy, and as a creative energy.

We are aware that it is still unusual for same-sex couples to be openly part of a religious order and community as fully accepted members, and for a religious order to view their way of life as an integrated life-path.

In some countries there is much debate about 'gay marriage'. The disagreement is not only over whether same-sex partnerships should be legally defined or not, but also about the form these partnerships should take and what this 'vessel' should be called. In the USA many gay and lesbian groups are campaigning for marriage to be an option for same-sex partners. While a few European countries tend towards the same direction, the majority – including Britain – have adopted special same-sex partnership laws. In Europe queer people hold differing views about these two options. In fact, my partner and I ourselves disagree on some aspects of this topic. Emanuel is strictly against taking the 'marriage route' because he sees it as a special historical arrangement for heterosexuals and feels that we gay and lesbian people should devise our own form of partnership. This view is, of course, influenced by our native German language, where the words for marriage and married couple ('Heirat', 'Ehe', 'Ehemann', 'Ehefrau') have a stronger heterosexual flavour than in English. While I agree that in many countries a same-sex partnership law might be the more realistic and therefore wiser step, in the end the question remains: Why not open up the institution of marriage to same-sex couples?

Something to be said for this proposal is the fact that marriage has been in a constant state of change throughout its whole existence. Moreover, from a spiritual point of view the core intention of marriage is the same as that of a homosexual partnership. Let me illustrate the latter point: Emanuel and I have been living in community for many years with various straight couples, some with children, some without. All of them have considered themselves to be on a Christian spiritual path. Through comparison, discussions, and communal prayer and worship we have discovered that the basic issues of our relationship and theirs are virtually the same – trust, shared spirituality, a common vision as a couple, learning to listen to each other, and finding God's will for our personal lives and as a couple, to name just a few. So if it comes down to the same fundamentals, then why not call it the same thing?

Still, there are different roads to this end, and it's certainly not the name that is the most important issue. It is the content and the direction, and of course the legal rights and support, that count. Emanuel and I met in May 1986, we fell in love, and moved in together the next spring. We definitely wanted some kind of religious service and public expression of our commitment to our partnership. So we decided to organise a service of blessing.

On 8th October 1988 we celebrated the consecration/blessing of our partnership in the sanctuary of the community house of our order in Basel, Switzerland. We devised this service together with a pastor from the Reformed Church, but it had an ecumenical flavour. During the ceremony we made vows to each other in which we each expressed the intention and focus of our relationship:

Emanuel:
'Urs, I promise to love you, respect you, to support you in
your work, to sustain you in prayer. I promise to stand by
you in difficult times and to rejoice with you in good
times, with the help of our Lord Jesus Christ.'

Urs:
'Emanuel, I want to share my life with you, to be on the
path with you, to set off to new frontiers.
'I will do my best to see and live our relationship always
from my central relationship with Christ: to accept and
love you, even in dark times.
'I want to give you space to develop your abilities to the
full and to shower you with my gifts over and over again.'

As a practical example of what that means for a relationship, I
would like to continue to describe our own circumstances. We are
trying to shape our life partnership as a gay couple so that we
support each other in emulation of Christ. This happens through
talking, arguing, consoling each other and praying together. In
our partnership we are able to reveal ourselves to each other just
as we are. With this attitude we strive to accept and love each
other and ourselves. This unconditional love – which is something we could never experience to such an intensity in a normal
friendship – strengthens and nourishes both of us.

We want to live our partnership in a way that radiates vitality
outwards to others. This happens through our wholehearted and
profound connection and through the way that we complement/
supplement each other and challenge one another.

Our shared and lived sexuality is obviously totally discon-
nected from procreation but nevertheless we experience tenderness and sexual intimacy as life-enhancing forces. In bodily,
corporal love, in intercourse, we experience a deep connectedness with each other and, ultimately, also with the cosmos and
with God. In orgasm we experience ecstasy, and are strengthened by the tenderness and the warmth of each other's bodies.
Through our physical embrace we gain energy. We want to put

this energy to the service of our fellow human beings and the whole of creation.

The following areas of practical service are close to our hearts:

- Hospitality, accepting others and making them feel welcome
- Openness to and solidarity with outcasts in our society
- Engagement in spirituality and social matters
- Commitment to integrating spirituality and sexuality, and engaging with other queer people and their friends to work for justice, respect and full acceptance for gays and lesbians in church and society.

Through the power of our relationship we experience a greater openness and freedom than we would alone. We see that a function of our partnership is to serve those around us and all creation. As a couple, we want to live and convey spirituality. Through our shared journey we develop a spirituality that is more than just our individual spirituality. The relationship with God that we share should be infectious. In that way our partnership can be an inspiration for other lesbians and gays and even for heterosexual couples.

What I have said here about complementarity and challenge in our relationship is a process through which we grow personally and continue to learn. We trust that what is given to us may develop and that, as a result, new life will grow in us and through us.

It is helpful that there are so many examples of committed gay and lesbian couples, and it is likely that such people will become even more visible. While the press certainly highlights celebrity couples like Elton John and his partner David, it is important that other same-sex couples who are not famous also get more of their due. Regarding same-sex couples who see themselves as being on a spiritual journey, there are some books published that celebrate their love with texts, poems and photos. There is also more and more research being done about couples from previous centuries, for example John Boswell's startling book about ancient rituals for same-sex couples.

Another interesting idea that I sometimes contemplate is that while straight men search for the feminine in their female partners, and straight women search for the masculine in their male partners, we queer couples – being of the same sex – have to search for the other polarity within ourselves. This gives us a profound insight into these energies and we can share this understanding with others.

Religious groups, of whatever kind, can only profit from a full and honest inclusion of same-sex couples. To finish this section, I quote again from the statement of the order to which my partner and I belong:

In the last few decades some religious orders have opened themselves up to include both sexes and (different sex) married couples and traditional families. In a similar way, the Friedensgasse has been one of the pioneer orders in opening up to gays and lesbians who are honest about their sexual orientation and who want to develop their unique potential for the benefit of the whole community.

Lesbians and gays who accept their homosexuality– whether they are single or in a committed partnership – will usually not parent or raise any children. As with child-less heterosexuals, this gives rise to a potential for cultural and social engagement. A religious order and community provides a framework in which this energy can be used to beneficial effect.

Because of their special sensibility towards disadvantaged people, many homosexual men and women are predestined to be active in the area of service in society, and in communal life they are often sensitive and tactful toward others.

Living together in community – or even just the fact of membership of heterosexuals and homosexuals in the same order – is a witness for society and the church that reconciliation is possible and that differences in sexual orientation are not a threat but a means of enrichment and a demonstration of diversity.

> *The partnership status in our order has in our opinion a prophetic dimension. It shows that same-sex couples can have a place in religious communities and orders. It visibly demonstrates the fact that the church and the world are much richer when gays and lesbians are permitted to be open about their way of life. Many homosexual people long for constructive relationship role-models. Life partnership can encourage them to engage in committed long-term relationships in a communal context. As homosexuals are still suppressed, ostracised and stigmatised in many cultural settings and classes of society, faith communities and religious orders that include gay and lesbian people as equal members provide a means of healing and reconciliation.*

In accord with this, the priest blessed us in the above-mentioned service for our partnership with the following words:

> *We ask you, God, the spring of life, we ask you, our brother Jesus Christ, we ask you Holy Spirit, God in us: Accompany Urs and Emanuel on their journey, help them to develop their friendship and use the opportunities that their crises will offer so that their gift which you have given them can blossom more and more; for your glory and to their joy. Bless their partnership and let it endure. Help them to let go and to die to their individual selves, to trustfully fall into your earth so that their life together can bring forth fruit. God, be the axis around which they revolve, be the spring from which they drink, be the joy for which they search. And the Lord bless you and protect you!*

These texts are reworked and extended from a short chapter I wrote with my partner for another book: Catherine & Pierre Brunner-Dubey: *Kraftvoll einkehren*. Lucerne 1996.

QUESTIONS

If you live in a partnership, how do you define yourself – individually and as a partnership – in spiritual terms? How do you live a spiritual life together?

As a couple, how do you share your spiritual life? Do you meditate or pray regularly together or discuss theological questions? Do you feel able to challenge each other on spiritual issues?

If you don't have a partner, are you able to live some of the qualities mentioned in this chapter with other people? Do you see your single status or celibacy as a gift?

If you are unhappy because you long for a partner, what steps can you take to find a spiritual-minded friend or partner?

SUGGESTIONS

If you have a partner, write down all the gifts you receive from your relationship with her or him. Maybe you will want to invite your partner to do the same and then discuss it together.

Select a nourishing gay spiritual book and read it together for common reflection on your life and partnership.

If you are single, take a look at your circle of friends and also at gay and lesbian literature and write down names of queer people who are single or who live in partnership, whom you admire or at least regard as good examples. Make a list and write down the qualities that are important for you.

EXERCISE

Guided meditation - The blessings of our lifestyle.

In the Jesuit Ignatian tradition of spiritual exercises there is a form of biblical meditation or visualisation where one actively meditates while reflecting on stories in the Bible, especially those from the Gospels. The idea is to imagine yourself in an encounter with Jesus.

If you have a partner who shares your spiritual journey, you may of course do this exercise together.

Choose a story of an encounter with Jesus from one of the Gospels – for example, Jesus and the Samaritan woman, or one of the healing miracles. Use a story which speaks to you and makes visible the loving, healing, caring side of Jesus. Read this story quietly several times and meditate on it for a moment. Be aware of the persons involved, of what Jesus says, those whom he touches.

Now close your eyes and imagine you are watching this scene; you are watching it from nearby. How do you feel? What do you notice? How does Jesus show his love? Depending on the scene he may also be angry at the hypocrisy and legalism of the Pharisees, the religious fundamentalists of their time. Give your imagination free rein: maybe you see the scene in its historical setting, with people dressed as they were 2000 years ago, or maybe everything looks very contemporary.

The scene that you read in the Bible has played out in your imagination and now you have the chance to meet Jesus yourself. Imagine yourself – alone or with your partner – approaching Jesus. Feel the love, the compassion, that flows from him. Possibly you see a white holy light surrounding his body. You now have time to tell Jesus your concerns and explain where you are at this point in your life. If you have a partner, share with Jesus what the gifts have been in your partnership, how you live the values of the Gospel in your home and outside of it, how you serve the world as a couple. If your relationship is going through a crisis, you may talk about this too. If you are single or celibate, you may (depending on your situation) speak about your disappointments in relationships, your yearning for a partner, your possible sexual confusion, or what being celibate means to you.

Be aware of how Jesus reacts: maybe he just listens; maybe he shares his wisdom and love; or maybe he hugs you or gives you a healing touch.

After you have finished sharing your thoughts and feelings, now get in touch with your hopes, wishes and aspirations for the future, either as a single person or as a couple. Ask Jesus now for strength and wisdom for your life. Ask him to bless you in whatever situation you are in. If you are alone or part of a community, ask him to bless your journey in this setting. If you are a couple, ask Jesus to bless you as partners of love, that your relationship may grow and be a loving witness in the world. Imagine how Jesus lays hands upon you and blesses you.

Be sensitive to the way you experience this blessing. Be open to the healing touch, to the power of the Holy Spirit that is within you.

It is now time to say goodbye in your imagination, knowing that you can meet Jesus again at any time. Open your eyes.

In order to deepen this experience, you might like to play some mellow, moving music that may encourage you to dance slowly in your room, alone or with your partner.

It might be useful to writes notes about this experience and share them with your partner or with a spiritual director or a trusted friend.

PRAYER

Christ,
Wherever two people love each other honestly,
You are present in that love.
We thank You for every couple that understands their relationship
as a gift from You.

We pray for couples that have to fight for their relationship
because of injustice, persecution and discrimination.
May You be present in their suffering and their struggles.

We pray for every new love found,
every new relationship started,
that it might blossom.

We ask for Your presence with Your healing hand
wherever there is conflict or separation.

We ask for strength and hope for gays and lesbians
who search sincerely for a partner
and for those who have consciously chosen
the path of being single or celibate.

Challenge us,
make our lifestyles vessels of love and peace
that reverberate in this world
which is in so much need of these qualities.

Amen

Six

Wounded Healers

The main focus of this book is the potential of homosexuality, and the opportunities it provides for personal growth and spiritual development. But still we are all aware that in the lives of gays and lesbians, even in today's progressive societies, woundedness is part of the reality too.

I hope that I have made it very clear in this book that I do not see gay and lesbian people as victims. Too much emphasis on victimhood lends strength to the other polarity, that of 'perpetrator' or oppressor. But I know that being wounded is inevitably a theme at some point in the lives of gays and lesbians. It is important to find a creative and healing way to deal with this part of our experience. In particular, I have met many religiously associated lesbians and gays who, because of condemnation from their churches, have allowed their self-expression and development to become blocked by grudges and frustrations. This is especially visible in men and women who struggle with fundamentalist Christian, Jewish or Muslim backgrounds.

But being wounded is not the end of it. Without exception everybody gets wounded at some point in life. Gay and lesbian people are of course especially vulnerable to homophobic attacks. But these do not have to result in lifelong suffering. There are ways of overcoming such things and being healed. We may even grow as a result of the experience to the point where it helps us to become healers ourselves.

Let's start with my own experience of being wounded as a gay man: The subject of homosexuality was totally taboo when I grew up in the 1960s and 1970s, at least in my family and school system. One didn't talk about same-sex love. The issues were ignored and there was a general expectation that everybody would turn out to be heterosexual. I became aware of my first homosexual feelings at the age of about 12, and a year or so later I saw the word 'homosexual' for the first time, in a TV magazine. As I didn't know what it meant, I checked in a dictionary and realised that I had the feelings described – but they were explained in pathological terms. I got the impression that the way I felt wasn't welcomed in this world and that there was something wrong with me. In my later teenage years and early twenties I became aware that in fundamentalist circles love between people of the same sex was condemned as sick, sinful, perverse or even demonic. I had two major experiences as a result of this attitude. At 23 I had to leave a theological seminary because it was discovered that I was gay. A year later I lost my job at an evangelical youth hostel for the same reason. As a consequence I took my leave of this conservative environment and continued my life journey with expanded theological horizons. But I soon realised that I could not just put those years of homophobic oppression away like an old book. A change on a mental level is not everything. Painful emotions, feeling and memories don't just disappear.

As a result of these life challenges I embarked on a process of questioning, discussion, debate and reorientation. I underwent various forms of psychotherapy where, among other issues, my wounds had their place. Looking back on my own and other people's experiences, I have come to the conclusion that for many lesbians and gays with a painful homophobic past some form of therapy may be necessary to bring about a process of healing.

Gay theologian Patrick W. Collins describes this process in an unpublished manuscript with the title *The Gay/Lesbian Wound.* (I will refer more to this in the chapter 'Coming In'.) He talks about the Christian mystic Thomas Merton:

Thomas Merton was deeply aware that God deals with human beings in and through their vulnerability, their wounds. It is at the point of what may appear to be one's powerlessness that divine power can act to make one whole. Heterosexist and homophobic assumptions and attitudes have created what has been termed 'The Gay Wound' - i.e. internalised homophobia. Guy Baldwin has said: 'At this time in history, homophobia is the single most defining element in gay consciousness.' (Baldwin in Thompson in Gay Soul, *p.190) Gays are socialised to imagine, feel, act and be different by straights who, in the past, have set the standards for 'normal' sexual orientation and interpersonal relationships. Environments and structures established by society and church have implanted within gay people a sense of being a misfit and an alien. This, in turn, can create a profound self-loathing in the gay soul which very often leads to self-destructive behaviours and the unhealthy stereotypic acts which negatively characterise the gay population among straights ... Yet such suffering can become the gateway to deeper truth and healed wholeness.*

(Collins, p.5)

Andrew Harvey, as a present-day contemplative writer and gay mystic, supports this view. He talks about the transformation of our pains:

From the deepest wound of my life grew its miraculous possibility. [...] Had I not been so wounded, I wouldn't have constantly hungered and searched, certainly not with the intensity that I have.

(Gay Soul p.51)

[...] Examining the wound is a preliminary and very important stage for entering the divine fire, just as the log itself is penetrated by the flame, crackles in that union, and then sinks into a softer, sweeter union before it becomes ash. Everyone who is destined to have a spiritual transformation comes to the journey with a wound (as large as God. They have to, to go through it.) Very few people are going to undertake the massive stripping it entails unless there is something tremendously painful urging them on. There are very few people who become advanced mystics because they simply feel happy on Sunday afternoons.

(Gay Soul, p.54)

He goes on to cite Ram Dass as a brilliant example of the many gay men who have inspired the spiritual movements of our day. Harvey points out that Ram Dass has used the fact of his gayness in the most creative and moving ways to communicate the highs and lows of the spiritual path. He seems to have no fear, and people sense this. However, Harvey states that there are many other gay men who are spiritual leaders exactly because they have suffered from the limitations of society. Having fought hard to transcend those restrictions within their own being, they have become better qualified to be spiritual pioneers. In effect, the larger the wound, the greater the opportunity.

The awareness that every one of us has a healing centre in the depth of our being is of paramount importance. There is a divine core in us that cannot be harmed by all the hurt that we receive on the personality level. This awareness can help us avoid defining ourselves as victims.

From a broader perspective, the hurts and wounds which we have experienced are not just individual, but also have a collective dimension: I argue that we are consciously or unconsciously connected with our gay and lesbian community – or tribe could be another name – of the present and past, on all continents. Ten thousand of us were murdered by the Nazis in concentration camps. On this planet, millions of lesbians and gays are still told that they are not allowed to exist the way they are. Even now, in many countries, homosexual people are persecuted, attacked, put into prison or even tortured and murdered. In extreme Muslim countries (like Saudi Arabia or Iran) the death penalty is still the lawful punishment for homosexual intercourse. While I was writing the original German version of this book, 52 gay Egyptians were put on trial and condemned to several years of imprisonment. Some of them were mistreated or tortured. Their only 'crime' was that they had organised and gone to a gay party. Meanwhile, we continue to buy oil from Saudi Arabia and Western tourists flock to Egypt instead of putting pressure on these countries.

This all is part of today's reality as much as the wide acceptance of homosexuality in countries like Holland and Denmark. We are not yet totally free from the danger of right-wing extremism or even fascism. The Vatican still publishes ugly homophobic statements, condemning gays and lesbians and forcing them out of church jobs. The fundamentalists on the Protestant side still tell lies and use psychological violence and religious abuse – for example, in their 'counselling' they try to foster guilt feelings and change people's sexual orientation.

You may have experienced some or all of this, depending on where you live and what your background is. What effect does it have on you as a gay man or a lesbian woman? When I hear such homophobic news, my immediate reaction is often to get angry or aggressive, or to feel fearful.

In addition to therapies, self-help groups and talking circles, I consider meditation and ritual the most helpful to deal with our inner wounds and to help us find our inner strength and freedom. Since 1988 I have meditated regularly in the Zen or contemplative traditions. A few years back, while taking part in a contemplation week, I went through a special stage of healing. By experiencing backache while sitting in meditation that week I got in touch with the pain of my soul. Although I tried to suppress this pain at first, I realised during the week how important it is to allow, tolerate and accept.

By acceptance I don't mean a masochistic search for pain! Acceptance means saying 'yes' to what is. This applied as much to the pain caused by my homophobic experiences, which I experienced again during this contemplation week, as to my physical pain. I let the pain be and I continued my meditation session. I said yes to all that is, and over and over again let everything go by breathing it out. I felt a sense of freedom arise from the depth of my being.

In the intervals between those meditation sessions the idea kept coming into my mind of accepting my various pains or wounds as 'brothers' and 'sisters'. In a visualisation I asked those different 'siblings' what kind of gifts they brought to me out of my woundedness. I took a notebook and wrote down: Generosity and a broad perspective. About my wounds resulting from homophobia I wrote: Love for sexuality, engagement in working for the dignity of lesbians and gays.

It was important for me to integrate those messages into my life. My wounds increased my sensibility. They taught me to honour the diversity of human beings, to get involved with and for people at the edge of society and to engage passionately for the freedom of humanity.

My roots in the Christian tradition helped me to come to terms with myself and to venture close to the pain of my wounds. The love of Christ and the experience of his presence were the foundations where the healing process could start. Becoming whole and growing into the possibilities of one's life is a lifelong process, and in this process I can experience my woundedness, my hurt feelings and my pain as a doorway to God, as a place in myself where the grace of God is at work.

I repeat this important advice: meditation and ritual are very useful tools for dealing with our hurt feelings, pain and wounds. You will find a suggested basic meditation exercise at the end of this chapter. I also want to emphasise that the Christian tradition offers perspectives on becoming mature and whole, as I will show in a later chapter, 'The Way of Christ'.

I wrote this part of the book during Holy Week. For over ten years I had actively taken part in the procession of the Way of the Cross through the city of Basel. We stop at various places in this Swiss city to remember different causes of pain and agony. Two people take turns to carry the large wooden cross from station to station till this Way of the Cross ends at a Protestant or Catholic city church, where the cross is set on the floor. Many small candles are placed around the cross and people can come forward for silent prayer.

At the stations along the procession route through the city centre all kind of different issues are raised: environmental concerns, xenophobia, sexual abuse of children, AIDS, etc. Once I was in charge of such a station outside a gay bookshop. I was responsible for the subject of violence and discrimination against lesbians and gays. It was not only a touching moment for the participants, the majority of whom were heterosexuals, but also an important act for me as a gay man. It was a public acknowledgement, in a spiritual context, of injustice against gays and lesbians as part of growing whole and as a testimony to our fight to give dignity to all aspects of human life.

That is one of the reasons why I believe that homosexual people are of great value to society, including religious institutions. I am curious to see what yet unknown power of change, unity and love will be available for the world, when people of all sexual orientations unite on this journey of reconciliation and salvation.

To experience justice – To promote justice

Justice is an important aspect of the guidelines of the order to which my partner and I belong. Justice in this context has, of course, nothing to do with punishment or hate for those who have done wrong. Justice, for us, is a road to a greater humanity and respect for all of creation.

During a training session held by our order we did a visualisation exercise on the theme of justice. In the first part, we considered the question: Which injustice within the human family touches me most at this moment and how has this injustice had an effect on the people involved? In the second part of the exercise, we opened ourselves to the presence of Christ and to seeing what new dimension can be realised from this point of view. To conclude this second part, we asked ourselves a personal question: What could be our own next step to greater justice?

On this particular evening in this exercise I envisioned the situation of homosexual people in countries like Iran where they are threatened with the death penalty, and countries where homosexuals may lose their jobs or end up in prison. I even thought of Switzerland, where in spite of all the improvements there is still discrimination when it comes to the church. Nor was it difficult for me to feel concern about these injustices, because of my own experiences of discrimination. Moreover, on an intellectual level, I knew about the injustice that millions of gays and lesbians have to suffer in different parts of the world. On this evening, though, I opened up to a deeper level. I could touch my wound and feel the pain. I wondered what I could do to bring about greater justice in this specific context. I knew that I was already doing a lot in terms of workshops for gays and lesbians, such as my spiritual project for queer people. But I still felt very angry when I heard how so-called Christian and Muslim fundamentalists or secular right-wing extremists treat gay and lesbian people. What, for me, would be a big step toward greater justice?

As I turned inward to the presence of Christ, I became aware that the next step must happen within myself, as a reconciliation process with the enemy I felt inside me. The injustice that has wounded me in the form of dogmatism and homophobia is not something I have to suffer passively. It includes a gift for me. These wounds awaken in me a great measure of love for justice. I open up to the value of sexuality. If I accept these gifts, then I don't have to hate and try to destroy those homophobic people. If I accept my feelings of anger without suppressing them, if I forgive my enemy, then energy is set free within me for a strong engagement in working for justice. I am convinced that this inner process of unleashing justice within oneself helps to advance a change of consciousness in this world. Evolution towards greater justice involves us all and includes both inner and outer changes.

After the session that evening, I heard and felt in meditation and prayer: 'Live justice in yourself. Justice for all, space for everyone. Integrate everything and you will create space for justice in this world.'

QUESTIONS

How have you been hurt as a lesbian or as a gay man? To what extent are these wounds still open?

When you get very angry, what do you do with your anger?

What kind of 'gift' could your wounds carry for your own life and for that of others?

Are you in danger of remaining in a victim role as a consequence of injustice that you have suffered? How could you change or break out of this role and take full responsibility for your life?

How can you live in solidarity with persons or groups who are oppressed?

SUGGESTIONS

For a couple of years now many churches in Europe have followed the developments in other parts of the world in including and revisioning the issue of healing. It is being more and more acknowledged that the healing stories in the Bible, especially the ones involving Jesus, can no longer be dismissed as just outdated mythological images or symbolic tales but that they have to be taken seriously as a dimension of Christian spirituality. (For too long the gift of healing has been left as the domain of cults or fundamentalist groups who have tainted it with pressure, moralism, narrow-mindedness and simple stupidity like condemning homosexuality as an illness.) In Basel, where I come from, an ecumenical city-church project 'Offene Kirche Elisabethen' (St Elisabeth Open Church) organises healing services. Other churches like St James Piccadilly in London or groups like the Iona Community have a similar healing tradition and the list of churches that are discovering a genuine healing ministry is growing.

If you are aware of such a serious ministry of healing, get in contact with it and test it. Talk to healers, read intelligent books about the subject. Maybe a healer will be able to help you in dealing with your wounds. Or perhaps you yourself have a call or talent for healing that wants to be awakened, so that you too can be a channel for the divine healing power.

Get in contact with an Amnesty International subgroup for gay/lesbian issues. This offers you the chance to show your solidarity with lesbians and gays who suffer violence and oppression in this world. You can engage in various forms of non-violent action as suggested by Amnesty and you may be able to make a contribution to changing this situation.

EXERCISE

Healing visualisation exercise with painting

First organise a big piece of paper and pens, brushes and paint and put them down close to you. Sit in a comfortable position or lie down on the floor. Take a few deep breaths and relax your body. While staying fully awake, close your eyes and get in contact with the silence and peacefulness inside you.

Remember an experience where you were hurt as a gay or lesbian person; where you were discriminated against, despised or not taken seriously.

Let this situation play out in detail in your memory and again, for a moment, be part of it.

Be aware of your body. Maybe you feel a pain in a specific part of your body. Be aware of your thoughts and associations. What do you feel at the moment? What qualities do these feelings have for you?

Sense in which part of your personality this painful experience matters most and what the consequences were or still are in your life.

Ask your imagination to bring up out of your depths a picture or symbol of this homophobic experience. Just let go and see what comes up. Don't judge. Take the first image that materialises, even if you find it odd.

Memorise this picture or symbol and slowly open your eyes in your own time and become fully present again in your room.

Draw or paint the picture or symbol you received and look at it. Maybe you enter an inner dialogue with it. Ask it questions. Maybe you hear an answer inside of you.

Take a short break without getting distracted. Have a drink if you need to.

Return to your sheet. Look at it intensively once more and get in touch with your own feelings and thoughts, and how they change. Now turn your paper over and take a few deep breaths and let all those thoughts and feelings go. Get back into your lying or sitting position and close your eyes while remaining fully awake.

Now open yourself to the presence of the divine, the Christ in you. Do it by calling his name out loud or in silence. Visualise yourself taking in the bright light of Christ and letting it flow through your body. Remember the pledge of his special grace which is effective where we are weak and hurt and where we trustingly accept our weakness and vulnerability. Jesus says: 'Let my grace act in you, then my strengths are powerful in the weak.'

Try to become aware of which special gifts, qualities, strengths and sensibilities are awakening and want to evolve when you allow the merciful and healing work of Christ to happen within you. Now let a new image arise in you that symbolises the strength of Christ's grace in you: a picture, a symbol that shows you the opportunities and the potential that is within you.

After seeing this inner image as clearly as possible, open your eyes and draw or paint it on the blank side of your paper.

Look at your drawing or painting and see if it has a message for you. If so, write it down.

Look once more at both your drawings or paintings and observe what meaning those two images carry for you.

(This exercise was inspired by an unpublished guided meditation by Catherine Brunner-Dubey.)

PRAYER

Christ, You are a healer.
I ask that I may experience healing
and salvation in my life.
Let my wounds not hinder me
from venturing out always anew.
Show me the gifts
that lie in my woundedness and vulnerability.
Guide me to act with healing in this world.

Seven

Sexuality as a Source of Strength

In this chapter I try to clarify how sexuality can be experienced as a source of strength for ourselves, our partners, our relationships and our spirituality. In thinking about sexuality in a spiritual context, we gain insight into how we can deal with it in a responsible manner. I am aware that this is a complex issue on which much has already been written. All I want to do here is give some suggestions and inspirations for how to handle it in relation to the subjects that this book addresses.

The guidelines of the order to which my partner and I belong include a statement on sexuality:

If we observe the evolution of life and of humankind, then we will recognise our sexuality as a creative force which fosters new life and furthers evolution. Our sexuality is the power of encounter, of relationship, of union. Sexuality is the power of love in us. Our nature as human beings is profoundly determined by our sexuality. Our sexuality is an essential component of our personhood. Therefore it is extremely important to shape and mould our sexuality carefully to allow our true self to unfold and therefore to be open to the reality of Christ.

Many people in our times do not know how to express their sexuality. This uncertainty has to do with a change of our sexual sense, and with a further step in the evolution of humanity. [...] Humanity is now in the stage of Noogenesis, what de Chardin calls the evolution of the Spirit. Passing into this new chapter in our evolution means that our creative force is becoming capable of ever broader expression within the psychological-spiritual spectrum.

We are now in a transition period and we want to use this stormy epoch as a challenge to search for new forms and ways to mould and give expression to our sexuality so that Christ can evolve in us and so that our ability to love is deepened.

(Kraftvoll einkehren pp.82,83)

Realising that our sexuality is a source of strength has its consequences, no matter what one's sexual orientation, or whether one is celibate or lives a physically expressed sexuality. Of course, heterosexuality can also be a source of strength. But I imagine that gay and lesbian people will play a special part in times to come as humanity increasingly discovers and learns to deal with its sexual drive in a nourishing and strengthening way.

Several questions may help us clarify to what extent we already live a mature and productive sexuality:

- What motivates our sexuality?
- When we make love, what do we experience psychologically, mentally and spiritually?
- Does our sexuality nourish and empower us?
- Do we constantly seek sexual adventure? Are we in fact addicted to compulsive physical sex?
- Does our sexuality give us deep joy?
- How important is our sexuality to us?
- Can we feel the power of our sexuality beyond sex and partnerships, in different areas of our life?

Many gays and lesbians are not aware that sexuality, as I would define it, has three levels or layers. When I discovered this working model a few years ago, it immediately felt very liberating and helpful. It shed a new light on many things in my life and world-view.

The three levels of (homo-)sexuality:

3. Sexuality as a different kind of consciousness

2. Sexuality as same-sex love in relationship

1. Sexuality as sex drive and sexual encounter

SEXUALITY

AS A

SOURCE OF

STRENGTH

For me these three levels are connected, although not necessarily identical, to the three levels of human consciousness posited by the various traditions of transpersonal psychology, especially Psychosynthesis:

3. Higher consciousness (the Higher Self)
2. Middle consciousness (the personal I)
1. Lower consciousness

I'll go through these three levels individually and then as a whole, and I'll show how they can be viewed as a source of strength. Of course, within the confines of this book there is sometimes not enough space to do more than hint at certain aspects.

Sexuality as sex drive and sexual experience

The majority of people, when they hear the word sex or sexuality, still think of the physical sex act. This is probably even more true of men than women. A mutually fulfilling sexual experience can include, circumstances permitting, a deep feeling of happiness or even ecstasy, in the sense of merging and melting and being deeply moved.

I still vividly remember the time when I first came into contact with the gay movement in the late 1970s. I attended a gay conference, and listening to the speeches and group discussions, reading the flyers, information sheets and gay papers, I got the impression that much revolved around plain sex. Some of the extreme gay men were for the abolition of marriage. Every binding form of partnership between two lovers, especially gay ones, was seen as an 'assimilation' into heterosexual society. For many men in the gay movement at that time, the ideal was to have sex with as many attractive men as possible, as often as possible, with no commitment at all to any of them. Except on the part of some feminist lesbians, there was little recognition that this attitude – the reduction of other human beings to sex objects – was an exact replication of the male heterosexual stance in a patriarchal society.

In the meantime, over a quarter of a century has passed and many unexpected events, like the AIDS crisis, have occurred. The lesbian and gay movement has become mature and, more importantly, much more diverse. In Europe and other parts of the world this has been helped by the obvious relaxation in attitude towards gays and lesbians, which has not only allowed them to develop their self-esteem but has also massively opened up the range of places where the gay/lesbian community can meet in public, which in itself has encouraged the development of lasting relationships.

But in spite of all this development, am I wrong to assume that for a significant minority of gay men anonymous sex still plays a major role (in the form of pornographic material in magazines, in movies and on the internet, saunas as sex clubs, darkrooms, parks and toilets for cruising, sex parties etc)?

One finds hardly any articles or discussion about how a constant change of sexual partners affects one's soul, aura, and psychological and spiritual well-being over the years. It still seems to be taboo even to consider this question. The matter of what (safe-)sex can be, in a holistic sense, beyond using condoms and avoiding AIDS, is never raised. How can sex nourish the whole person? We are not just physical bodies! Even the issue of respectful distance and intimacy are often avoided in the gay press. Men who are total strangers, who may not even know each other's names and indeed may have no interest in each other at all apart from a genital one, touch each other's most intimate body parts. Someone once told me, in a somewhat vulgar exaggeration: 'Ordinary people shake hands, gays shake cocks ...'

Of course, one has to take the context into account. Heterosexual men are not all that different. It is estimated that in some African and Asian countries up to about 80% of men go to prostitutes. In the Western world too, there is no shortage of heterosexual sex-saunas and so-called massage parlours.

In fact, I would say that it is gay men who imitate straight men, rather than the other way around, when they reduce sexuality to a consumer product. As feminist lesbians already noted in the 1970s, many gay men are in danger of replicating the extremely promiscuous behaviour of straight men. This tendency has little to do with the sexual liberation of the 1960s. Male sexual behaviour has been cast in this mould for centuries – perhaps since the development of patriarchal society much farther back in the past. It is a delicate and complex subject but there is not the space to explore it here.

There remains a further question about the extent to which a disintegrated sexual identity and the narcissistic tendencies induced by a homophobic society give rise to impersonal sexual behaviour. A lack of self-esteem can lead to obsessive-compulsive behaviour. This often camouflages or conceals feelings of emptiness, longing or yearning, and the search for and the fear of intimacy.

In his books, John McNeill looks at yet more reasons for a sexual life being split off. Those who fail to take the first step of loving themselves are in danger of compensating through affairs or sexual encounters. Loving oneself is the basis for a healthy relationship. Self-hate has destructive consequences for one's sexuality. Could it be that this is the case with men who search for sex in dark places where they can remain anonymous? (see McNeill: *Glorious Freedom*, p.75)

The desire for sex is a powerful one, reflecting the energy bound up in our sex drive. If I try to describe this aspect of myself off the top of my head, the following images come up: glowing fire, lava, ecstasy and wildness. Every love relationship provides the opportunity to put this sexual power into an appropriate context: the space to live in intimacy, to experience playful energy, to touch each other both on the physical level and in the depth of one's being, to expand and melt in orgasm.

Sexuality as same-sex love – Love in relationship

The current debate, mostly in the Western world, about legal recognition of same-sex partnerships bears witness that more and more gays and lesbians live in committed long-term relationships. Religious lesbians and gays want to celebrate this commitment in a service of blessing.

In a partnership, sexuality includes personal aspects. Intercourse and tenderness are the language of love in relationship. Sexuality strengthens the bonds, offers mutual enjoyment and deepens intimacy between the two committed lovers.

If I make love with my partner, it's not just a 'release' of energy. On the contrary, our loving sexuality creates new energy. Sexuality energises – especially in a partnership. This is important to note, since it is often claimed that it is only in celibacy that sexuality can be transformed. For a few people lifelong sexual abstinence may be a real calling and an appropriate method of development. But this is not the only path of sublimation and transformation: I don't have to renounce physical love and orgasm with my partner if I want to experience my sexuality as a means of empowerment. My own experience, and that of many other people, is that intercourse can channel new energy. Making love can empower the couple and strengthen their lives and gifts.

In sharing my sexuality with my partner I open myself fully to intimacy. I'm not just physically naked but experience in a unique way the joining of our auras and the flow of energy between us. Tenderness creates a closeness that heals wounds, gives comfort and a sense of security, and encourages trust. In the many years of our partnership I have several times encountered sacred images connected with lovemaking, especially just after orgasm. Two I remember well are:

- The perception of an energy circuit between my life partner and myself: like a circle of bright energy passing through us, connecting us, and extending and expanding us.

- An imaginative insight into the creation story: As God created the cosmos He/She must have had an 'orgasm' too.

Emanuel and I want to use this energy wisely and powerfully in our life together. And we are not the only ones. Besides couples I know personally, I have read about others in a number of books where committed gay and lesbian couples describe their partnership. This touches me and makes me aware that the power of a relationship can produce an energy that resonates in creativity and engagement beyond the partnership itself.

Couples who discover their sexuality as a 'holy power' will use this energy in service to others and the world. Couples who are consciously on a spiritual path together will naturally want to celebrate their partnership with a service of celebration or union. Some may even go as far as to call it an exchange of marriage vows. Whatever the name, such a celebration offers the opportunity to express the intentions and goals of the relationship. This creates an energy field that nourishes both of them and the environment in which they live. More about this in the chapter on partnerships.

Sexuality as an alternative path of consciousness

I have described this aspect already in the chapters about the potential and the real, substantial skills of gay and lesbian people. My impression is that not much is yet known about this level of sexuality in the current lesbian and gay community. If this awareness breaks through in the next few years or decades, then there will be a renaissance of the gay and lesbian movement.

The essence of homosexuality is not in 'doing' but in 'being'. In the depth of our being we encounter the divine reality. God has no gender or sexual orientation. God is the source, the well. To stay with a similar image: Our homosexuality is like a river bed. To the extent that the river bed can influence the calmness, wildness, speed, form and depth of the water, our same-sex orientation can be a 'river bed' which influences our consciousness and spirituality. And this different consciousness is a gift for us and for the world. Homosexuality embodies a potential and along with that a reservoir of talents and opportunities.

Sexuality as a source of strength: integrating all three aspects

So far in this chapter, I have looked at the three aspects or levels of sexuality separately. But of course they belong together. Many queer people may not be aware of all the levels, especially the third one, or they may find themselves stuck at the first level. It's important not to suppress or deny any of these three aspects, not even the ubiquitous and often commercialised first level. The enormous power of the plain sex drive has to be taken seriously and integrated with the other two levels. Like a snake (for me a beautiful creature!) this coiled sexual energy must move 'upward' to the second and third levels, connecting them all. It's not possible here for me to go into the details of the fascinating Eastern concept of the kundalini, which is often symbolised by a snake, but if you can take the time to read serious books about it, it's worth the effort . You'll find too that from the Christian point of view there are crossover points with the idea of the pervading and penetrating ecstatic element of the Holy Spirit.

The integration of these three levels becomes a turning point and training ground for people who want to follow a spiritual path. Whether you are bisexual, homosexual or heterosexual, everyone is challenged on this path of sexual integration.

Of course, I am aware that there are many variations and shadings of sexual behaviour. There are not just, on the one hand, people who are celibate or in a sexually faithful partnership and, on the other hand, people who have sex with hundreds of anonymous sexual partners over the years. In reality there are many different sexual lifestyles in between – shorter personal sensual relationships or intimate friendships, which painfully fall apart. Moreover, most people will not have their first sexual encounter with the person with whom they eventually form a lifelong partnership. A learning process of sexual experimentation may constitute the first step of their personal development.

Whatever the individual situation, in the end, all of us on a spiritual journey are called to decide on our sexual ethics and the partnerships we form out of the centre of our being, out of the 'Christ within'. It is not out of judgementalism or moralism but out of the liberating divine spirit that we make and live our decisions in freedom, with responsibility and dignity. Of course, sometimes we struggle and stumble on our way. We may make mistakes. But from these experiences we learn and are therefore able to apply those lessons to our life.

How can we experience sexuality as a source of strength and nourishment?

Having given in this chapter some glimpses of my personal experience with my sexuality I want to share some insights from other lesbians and gay men:

- At one of the retreats for gay and lesbian people I regularly facilitate in Tuscany, a male participant of about 30 years old shared with me quite early in the week that so far he had only had sex in dark places (like so-called darkrooms in gay saunas or in public parks at night), usually without knowing the names of his partners or seeing their faces clearly. I listened to him and perceived his pain, sensing his helplessness and questioning. Of course, in my approach to listening and counselling, any moralising and put-down are out of place. We talked about his issues and I proposed in particular that he should open up in contemplation to the divine dimension, God's presence in himself: to be present in prayer, to let go in meditation and to take part freely in group processes. During this week something happened to him. He discovered a new, holistic love for his body, he was able to accept his homosexuality much more easily and he developed a passion for meditation. He became strongly aware of his own dignity and that of the other members of the retreat group. He discovered a desire to make a connection between the sex act and friendship. I stayed in occasional contact with him after this week and he continued on a spiritual path. Soon he found a boyfriend. Even though this relationship ended after about a year, he had created an important experience which fostered his further personal development and helped him to mature.

- Emanuel and I visited a gay couple we had known for a while. After they had shown us their beautiful house in a small Swiss town and we were enjoying dessert following a marvellous supper together, the discussion became increasingly personal. Eventually, the two men, both in their thirties, who had been living together for about four years, started asking us personal questions about our attitude to sexuality in our partnership. One of the main questions was about our view of sexual faithfulness. They asked this because they were irritated by the values and assumptions expressed in gay media and literature, which often model or even recommend 'open' – sexually unfaithful – relationships as a healthy and constructive long-term behaviour for couples. (The straight press usually takes the same approach: infidelity, affairs and partner swapping are discussed in all their sensational detail.) We got into an in-depth discussion with this gay couple and explained why sexual fidelity matters to us, how we would honestly deal with possible lapses and how we maintain our approach in a sexually very permissive society which often reduces sex to a consumer product.

• The following testimony was written by a lesbian friend of mine. Since she is employed in an important position in the Roman Catholic church and would risk her job by coming out in a publication, she has decided to use a pseudonym:

Living alone as a lesbian woman, connecting spirituality and sexuality

This title alone may cause a reaction: Can living alone as a lesbian woman and connecting spirituality and sexuality all go along together? Many of my friends, the majority of them women, would say: never! And yet it works. Moreover, it is a viable human lifestyle leading to a fulfilling life. It is my journey to a full life.

At the end of my twenties I had my coming out; that was about 18 years ago. This finally made me realise why I never really found men attractive and never had a boyfriend. When I fell in love, it was always with women – but always with the 'wrong' one. Those women didn't want anything from me. Was it just bad luck? Or might there have been something else ... ?

Over the years I fought inner fights with the church and with God and finally came to the deep conclusion that God created and wanted me the way I am, including being lesbian. This was the next major step. But up to a point it was just a theoretical knowing; I was very convinced of it but something was missing, I didn't fully feel and experience God's love. But that was soon to change: While on a silent retreat (Ignatian exercises) I had the experience that 'someone' was starting to get interested in me – yes, was even flirting with me. Flirting is not a word that I would have connected with God, but that's how it was, undeniable for me! And in the following years my relationship with God got deeper and closer. For me, this is something very real and in no way religious babble, even if it may sound strange to many people. The critical point is whether this experience has life-enhancing or life-damaging consequences. This relationship enabled me to take enormous steps of maturation in my personality which were also experienced as very healthy by other people around me.

Therefore I am convinced that this is something very real, something initiated by God, coming from God. And then the theme of celibacy became my focus. Could it possibly be that my life-path is not to live in partnership with another woman, but to live alone as a single person. The crucial point is not the emphasis on being alone, but engaging in a deeply fulfilling relationship with God. So fulfilling that it excludes a deep and committed human relationship or partnership. Of course I do not judge this in any way. The conclusion that a marriage or partnership is a one-of-a-kind relationship, and therefore cannot be lived with another person, does not include a judgement either. And again we have the criterion: Does this decision lead to a fuller life or is it an escape from life? I have to answer that I have been much more open to other people and to the variety of possible forms of relationships and lifestyles. And my love relationship with God gains constantly in depth and vitality.

This is my point about spirituality. Now, does this mean that sexuality has become irrelevant to me? No. This relationship with God has a strong sexual, corporal component. It is one thing to experience the closeness of God on the emotional level with a deep connectedness and unity. But in rare moments I also feel it with my body: As a human person I am not just soul and spirit – I am also body. This corporal aspect of my relationship with God is evidence for me that I am not suppressing my sexuality but that I live as a whole human being, as a complete woman, in this relationship. The phrase from the Gospel of John has become reality for me '... and the word became flesh'.

What I have tried to describe here is certainly not a 'normal case' of living alone, of being single, but rather an exception or a special gift. But maybe this example will serve one or another reader as an inspiration to regard being single not as a deficiency or a lack, but as a potential gift, and to question whether getting a partner is really what one wants for one's life or if it may rather be staying or becoming celibate.

Maria F.

In the spiritual centre in Tuscany of the ecumenical community to which my partner and I belong, we regularly celebrate liturgies on different subjects. On Saturdays it's the liturgy 'Celebrating our sexuality'. In it we acknowledge joyfully and with thankfulness our sexual energy, in prayer before God. The liturgy was written by the founders of the order and is included in their published book. (Pierre & Catherine Brunner-Dubey: *Die Quelle in Dir darf singen*, pp.165/166)

It may seem strange at first that a liturgical prayer has our sexuality as its focus. In order to understand this, we must see the larger picture, in which human sexuality has its place and meaning.

This larger context is the story of the universe, the unfolding and the evolution of consciousness. We start with the knowledge that the love of God is the origin of all life. This love is revealed and differentiated through the unfolding of evolution. As human beings we have a special task and place: it's our role to experience, to express and to give shape to this love through the differentiation of consciousness.

Love, as seen by Teilhard de Chardin, is the creative power of the universe, which drives evolution and has as its goal the revelation of Christ in his universal form, as the beginning and end of creation. In this way our gender and sexuality are the primary expression of our capability to love. This creative power serves the unfolding of life and spiritual development.

If we consider the situation of our planet and the global threat to life and also consider our attitude towards sexuality, then there is no doubt that we are called to seek new forms of expression for our sexual energy and power.

This binds us to ethics and to a responsibility in interpersonal relationships. There is an ethic of evolution, in which all powers are directed toward a higher goal, namely the unfolding of Christ's presence in us and the world. Sexuality and spirituality belong together.

If we dedicate a liturgy to our sexuality, we do so in the knowledge that the history of Christendom has contributed significantly to making a taboo of it, to oppressing and suppressing our sexuality. As a result, many people are unsure, wounded and disoriented in relation to their sexuality.

In prayer we open ourselves to discovering new ways to give shape to our sexuality, both in a partnership and in all other relationships. In this way our ability to love is deepened and can become an authentic expression of our love for God and God's love for us.

In prayer for reconciliation with the history of the Christian church, we seek for reconciliation between homosexual and heterosexual people, and between men and women, and we also seek for reconciliation with the dark side of our sexuality.

In prayer we celebrate the body. In prayer we conse-crate our sexuality to Christ and allow our self to be trans-formed, so that our sexuality may more and more serve the all-pervading presence of Christ.

Whatever changes in our consciousness through this liturgy can help us to live new ethics on a daily basis. For example, this can mean that we become capable of deciding whether to enter a partnership or to remain celibate, or that we say yes to masturbation as an expression and means of love, or that we decide to exercise abstinence as a way to self-realisation.

This liturgy is written in an inclusive language and it is hoped that it will open the way to other prayers and forms of worship that acknowledge humans as sexual beings. There are also other exercises and tools for learning to experience sexuality as a holistic source of strength.

What can I do on a practical level to experience my sexuality as a source of strength, empowerment and nourishment?

Here are some down-to-earth simple exercises and further suggestions:

- Focus your awareness on your genital area. It may or may not happen that this gives rise to sexual fantasies. Whatever your impulses, visualise your sexuality as an energy; render this energy into colour, like orange or red or whatever comes up. Now imagine how this energy fills your pelvic area and moves up your spine all the way to the crown of your head.

- Lie down on the floor, the sofa or the bed in a room where you are alone. Lay your one hand on your genital area and the other on your heart. Feel the connection between those two centres of your being. Without making any judgements, see what happens. Let the energy flow between those centres and be aware of the connection.

- Draw your sexual organs or model them in clay, the inside or outside part, whatever you feel drawn to. Enjoy doing it without 'censorship'. For example, as a man you may want to make a huge phallic symbol.

- Get yourself interested in chakra (energy centre) work. There is now a great body of literature about this in English and a wide choice of seminars and individual training available. Take a look on the internet. Maybe you will feel drawn to that kind of energy work as a tool to further integrate your sexuality as well as other aspects of your life.

- Write or pray aloud sensual prayers. Tell God in personal prayer your erotic desires, thank Her for your body, praise Him for your genitals. Also include your wishes for a partner in your prayers.

- Whoever follows 'the road less travelled', who is on a serious spiritual journey, comes to a point where it is helpful to have a therapist or spiritual director, or at least to reflect on your journey as a spiritual and sexual being with a wise person whom you can trust.

- Read literature about sexuality and spirituality. You may be interested in Tantric literature too but look beyond books which reduce Tantra to stimulating sexual techniques. Seek out ones that encompass sexuality within a deeper and broader spiritual journey.

- If you have a lover or partner who is open-minded towards spirituality, try to pray with her or him. Why not also just give thanks for sex in the same way that you may say grace before eating a meal?

- Massage yourself or your partner regularly with body lotion or suitable oil. Be fully present in the massage and experience the touch with every cell of your body.

- If you choose masturbation as your regular or occasional sexual activity, try to include the whole of your body and your full attention. Be aware of your breathing and your sexual energy. Touch more then just your genitals so that this energy can spread to other parts of your body before you experience orgasm. In this way your experience of masturbation can be more holistic and sensuous.

- Put a spiritual icon in your bedroom or the room where you usually have intercourse or masturbate, to remind you of the connection between sexuality and spirituality.

- If you live in a committed relationship, discuss this chapter with your partner to encourage an exchange of views about your sexuality from a spiritual point of view.

Before I end this chapter with some questions, more practical suggestions and a visualisation exercise, I want to share a personal prayer experience. A few years ago I went to the sanctuary in our house and sat down on my meditation cushion in front of an icon of Jesus. I started praying spontaneously. By letting go and opening myself up to the divine Source, I asked questions about how to handle (homo-)sexuality in an empowered way. I received an answer to my prayer and I spontaneously and fluently wrote down what came up. Try to read it with the heart, in a mystic frame of mind:

You gay and lesbian people are My specially loved divine children, often unrecognised by the established religions, but endlessly in My good hands, in My wide and eternal truth and reality.

As I created your different consciousness, I had this in mind for the whole world. Serve the whole of creation with your special consciousness.

As I created the male and the female bodies I didn't limit my intention to heterosexuality and reproduction. I created the human body as woman and man in its sensuous beauty in a way that also a man can enjoy a man and a woman can enjoy a woman.

I created love as much for lesbian and gay people as I did for the rest. Live in relationships. Same-sex couples create energy. Be faithful. Serve the world.

Let your sexuality flow and focus on one point. Share and live it with your partner and beyond this as an energy that serves the world. Bundle this sexual energy like a laser beam, like a river that drives the dynamo of a power station.

Let your sexuality flow through your body, up the spine to your head, into your heart and through all your chakras.

Imagine how this same energy and power flows to places in the world where there is suffering, for example to countries where gay and lesbian people are oppressed, such as Iran.

Sexuality, listen! You open doors, you spread yourself out, vigorous, focused and full of relish. Fire aspect of the Holy Spirit. You are the energy which connects every aspect of being and streams through consciousness and broadens it.

The sexuality that I created: original, one of a kind, bewitching, beguiling, connecting. My fire that burns inside you.

Thank Me – I thank you. Live from the consciousness that you are My beloved daughter, My beloved son. This consciousness carries you and moulds you in working with your sexuality.

QUESTIONS

Do you know a mature person you can talk to about your sexual ethics and experiences?

What do the following phrases and words mean to you with regard to your sexuality: source of strength, exchange of energy, holiness, respecting one's partner, loving one's own body, the body as the temple of the Holy Spirit? Write down what comes up for each suggestion and reflect on it.

Take a close look at your own life to see where you are living and integrating the three levels of sexuality. Is there part of your life and sexuality where you want to grow?

SUGGESTIONS

Photocopy the pages in this chapter which include practical suggestions to help you to experience your sexuality as a source of strength and nourishment and put them on a wall in your bedroom where they are visible. Or write down the points which inspire you on a separate piece of paper.

Write a short memoir with the title 'My sexuality and me'. Look at your life from that angle. Write the story of your sexuality. Maybe you will discover what a great gift it is, or you will realise that your relationships always follow the same pattern and go wrong at the same point. Perhaps there will be issues you want to look at with a counsellor. Or perhaps you will discover the connection between your sexuality and your spirituality, or a calling to a celibate lifestyle, or the desire to find a new partner ...

EXERCISE

Sexuality as a source of strength

1. Lie down on a soft underlay and pillow on the floor or on a bed with a hard mattress. Ensure that your head is well supported and you can fully stretch out.

2. Close your eyes and allow your feet, legs, pelvis, back, spine, chest, shoulders, arms, hands, neck and head to relax. Become aware of your whole body as a physical totality.

3. Now direct your full attention to your genitals:
    * As a woman, become aware of your inner sexual organs; the ovaries, the Fallopian tubes, the uterus, the vagina, and the outer sexual organs, the labia and the clitoris.
    * As a man, become aware of your testicles with the various glands that are incessantly active within them, and your penis.

4. Be aware that as a man or a woman you are a sexual being. Acknowledge that your gay or lesbian sexuality makes a special contribution to your being human; that it further defines you as a unique woman or man.

5. Take some time to get into deeper contact with your sexual energy by concentrating on your genital area. Sense the energy, power and strength that reside there. Maybe you experience it as warmth, fire, a glow, lava, vibration or oscillation.

6. Whatever you feel and experience – whether the energy feels strong and powerful or weak, meek and quiet – welcome it as a part of you, as your strength and power to love and as a possible means of expressing yourself.

7. Now gather your sexual energy. Visualise it being compressed or condensed into a ball of energy. See it as an orange ball in the area of your genitals.

8. With fully conscious awareness, let this orange ball move upwards along your spine. Slowly guide it to your pelvis, to the

small of your back, up to your shoulder blades. Then let it move further upward between your shoulder blades to your neck. Now guide this ball further in your imagination up the back of your head to its crown. From there let it roll down over your chest to the solar plexus in the area of your stomach and further down over your navel, until the ball of energy finally arrives back in your pelvis. Give yourself enough time to rest and experience this orange ball in your pelvis.

9.   Now let this orange ball of energy burst open, so that its power and energy can spread out into your whole body. Notice how this energy fills every part of your pelvis. Allow it to spread into your abdomen and from there continue to flow up to the head, into your brain, filling all your millions of brain cells. Let this energy flow through your arms into your fingertips.Be aware of how the three levels of sexuality are full of this energy; from your genitals it has spread to your heart, and also to your consciousness. Notice how your body as a whole is full of this sexual energy; how it animates and invigorates you; and how this strength and power is flowing into every cell of your body.

10.   Acknowledge your sexuality as a source of life, as an expression of your ability to love, as a never-ending stream of strength and power within you. Acknowledge the divine grace which is being given to you along with your sexuality. Acknowledge Christ, God's creative force, in your sexuality

11.   Now slowly bring your awareness back to your room and, when it feels right for you, open your eyes. Be fully awake once more and present in the here and now.

(Free adaption of an exercise in *Kraftvoll einkehren*, pp.204–206)

PRAYER

God,
I am overwhelmed by the richness, strength, abundance,
complexity and versatility of your gift of sexuality.

Help me to deal with my sexual impulses, fantasies and desires
in such a way that I live my sexuality without being compulsive,
ruthless or inconsiderate, but with dignity, honest passion and true
surrender.

Help me to live my sexuality with my partner in a way that allows our
relationship to mature, so that we touch each other deeply in orgasm
and grow in tenderness.

If I don't have a partner and have a strong desire for a lover, be close
to me in this desire and searching, and when I feel alone.

If I am single, help me to decide whether to take part in sexual
encounters or whether total celibacy is appropriate and advisable.
Let me deal with masturbation with respect and imagination.

In my being gay, being lesbian, help me to be aware that I can serve
the world because I am different. May this consciousness and sexual
energy help to transform the world.

I thank you for the beauty, ferocity, ecstasy and joy of my sexuality –
for this energy that has allowed me to experience so much. Thank you
for this energy of life.

Eight

Coming In

The next step

In the order to which my partner and I belong, we say this prayer (written by a well known Swiss mystic five hundred years ago) before our morning contemplation.

Mein Herr und Mein Gott
Nimm alles von mir, was mich hindert zu Dir
Mein Herr und Mein Gott,
Gib alles mir, was mich führet zu Dir,
Mein Herr and mein Gott,
Nimm mich mir und gib mich ganz zu eigen Dir.

My Lord and my God,
Take everything from me that keeps me from you.
My Lord and my God,
Give everything to me that guides me to you.
My Lord and my God,
Take all of me and make me all your own.

Niklaus von der Flüh

From coming out to coming in

Much has been written about coming out. Being true to yourself and honest about what you are certainly has its spiritual aspects. Renowned gay Christian writer Chris Glaser wrote a highly recommended book with the title *Coming Out as Sacrament* where he makes the point that for gay and lesbian people the coming out process is a sacred event in itself. In this chapter I want to suggest that gays and lesbians on the spiritual path need to take a further step and enter yet a new dimension. As a few other gay spiritual writers have done before, I call this 'coming in'. Coincidentally a gay man called Tim Pickles wrote the following in an email to the members of the British gay spiritual organisation The Edward Carpenter Community, without being aware that at the same time (October 2004) I was working on the English edition of this book, *Coming In*:

The last two years for me have witnessed such huge change, that I am only just beginning to realise and appreciate the growth that has occurred. A remark by Alex Ramer has triggered this dawning awareness of a new phase in my life of 'Coming In', leading to perhaps the most satisfying and enriching period in my physical life so far.

The first few months after the long night of the separation from my partner was a period of deepening depression, leading to illness, hurt and withdrawal. Sickness, tablets, sleep all made little impact. It was nine months to a spirituality event that started the process of reclaiming my life, realising the radical changes that I wanted to make, and engaging in this journey.

Of course, the seeds have been there throughout my life: Quakerism, social justice, sexuality, self-belief, diversity, creativity, nothingness, awareness of soul, love, [...] and more. Over the past two years, this spirit journey has flowered – through reading, workshops, discussions, meditations, encounters, friendships, intimacies, and even physical injury. Together with close friends, this community has played a significant role in the process. The journey is giving me an awareness of my spirit home, of my distinct purpose in this queer tribe, of my differentness and uniqueness, of my role in being with and between others, of the value of my diffuse intimacies, of my connectedness with all other objects, of the constant transformation and re-birth that constitutes life and death, of diverse sexual expressions, of the peace and stillness at the inner core of being, of the noise within silence and the fullness of the space around, of letting myself just be, of the limitless power of my spirit essence. I'm beginning to appreciate that this is what Ramer meant by 'Coming In'. It's about Coming In to who we truly are as gay men.

Tim then continues to quote Ramer:

We're living on a two-way street and traffic is going in both directions. Coming Out is one direction. But there's another direction, which I call Coming In. Coming In to who we are, energetically, spiritually. Both directions are necessary, and both of them are true ... For many people. Coming Out is a sexual act. Coming In can include sex, but Coming In is about essence – not about experience.

(Alex Ramer, 1995, quoted in *Gay Soul*)

The weakness of many queer organisations is that they see the coming out process, and achieving a few rights, as the end of the road of liberation for LGTB people. But this is not our ultimate destination.

Coming out is the first and certainly an immensely important part of the journey to truth. But this coming out and 'fighting out' is not the whole journey. After undertaking the outer journey to the best of our ability, a new dimension awaits. We need to discover our true being and identity in our inner life; to make the journey to the centre of our soul, to discover our own core. This process of coming in can become a source of deep sustenance for our life.

Of course, this centring, this letting go, this finding of our spiritual path, is not exclusive to queer people. It is a universal phenomenon. However, the spiritual journey of gay and lesbian people distinguishes itself in some respects from the path of straight men and women. That does not mean that our sexual orientation is all-defining but it is one factor determining our identity and inner life. It underlies our perceptions and our approach to relationships.

Spiritual growth for same-sex-oriented people has two different, but not separate, aspects: coming out and coming in. These two seemingly opposite currents of inner energy have to be brought into synthesis. The coming out process that enables queer people to orient themselves toward their environment (in terms of the queer scene, the media, etc.) and to find their identity and true place in the world needs to be balanced by the journey of

coming in towards our inner space and working on our consciousness. Coming out and coming in complement each other.
Coming in has a lot to do with silence, contemplation and
letting go. (At the end of this chapter there is an introduction to
contemplation, together with instructions for doing it.) There is
a first dimension of coming in that is about retreat, about getting
involved in silence, becoming immersed in the depth of our own
being, experiencing the divine reality. Renewed by this inner
silence we are able to think, make decisions and take action.

But there is also a second dimension of coming in. The inner
spiritual journey eventually becomes an outer one as well which
not only disrupts homophobic patterns in our society but also
liberates us from the role expectations that dominate the
commercial lesbian scene and, even more so, the gay male scene.
As much as I am deeply thankful for the international gay and
lesbian movement, I cannot close my eyes to the fact that it also
incorporates some self-destructive patterns and has over-assimi-
lated the questionable values of wider heterosexual society.

I am aware that this shadow side of the LGTB community is a
delicate choice of theme. We all have a unique life story with a
joyful, bright side but also with a secret, painful side. It is justi-
fied to look not only at the bright side but also at the discredited
shadow side. Where there is much light, there is also shadow.

There is a further reason for the explorations that follow: I
hope they will communicate something to lesbians and gays who
have only recently become interested in spirituality, having
followed a different path from my own. I am sure that not all
readers by any means have had a life path similar to mine. They
may have grown up in a totally secular family or may have totally
broken with religion some time ago and are thus at a very different starting point.

Ever since I can remember, every day of my conscious life I
prayed in one way or another. I took for granted my connection
to Christ and to what is called the transpersonal dimension,
even if it was from a very childlike perspective. At the age of 18,
out of the blue, I had a groundbreaking, overwhelming spiritual

experience, where within a couple of hours I was blessed with a glimpse of the transformation of consciousness and my relationship with God. It was an extreme mystic experience of coming in. This had a lasting effect on my love for God, my faith and my balance of energy. Since then, by grace, I have been given a few more such life-enhancing experiences, where I have suddenly been overwhelmed by the love of God or have felt a life-changing unity with all that is.

In that same year, I started my coming out and found the courage to talk about my homosexuality with other people. In my personal life coming in and coming out were interwoven, so to speak. Even though I had much work to do to clarify and deepen my Christian faith, my theological direction and my same-sex orientation, I had had a taste of the divine presence quite early on, and felt a calling to strive towards God. So I did not throw faith or religious affiliation overboard, as understandably many queer people do, nor did I immerse myself unreservedly in the gay commercial scene.

By getting to know so many lesbians and gay men over the last 25 years I have realised that many journeys look very different from mine. Many people consigned the Christian faith to the rubbish heap during their teenage years or a little later, or were never consciously raised in a Christian context. The latter is now more and more common and our Western society is for the most part secularised. In 1970, in the Swiss city of Basel where I grew up, about 90% of the population belonged to a church. Thirty years later that was down to 50%. In Amsterdam, only 5% of the population now claim church membership. Many areas of Britain and Ireland show a similar trend. Of course, there are exceptions in the Western world, like parts of the USA, but a large number of people are estranged from traditional religion and that of course includes the gay and lesbian population. Many gays and lesbians have their coming out and then drift into the homosexual subculture or become active members of all kinds of LGTB groups and organisations. Some lesbians and many gay men then live their sexuality quite excessively, going to lots of parties, hanging around in bars or even taking drugs. The question, of course, is whether this is a passing phase of experimentation or a longer-lasting indulgence in the commercialised scene.

I have the feeling that there are some gay men and women who have had early deep spiritual encounters such as I had. But many other queer people begin to search for spirituality between the ages of 30 and 50. They have realised by this time that the standard gay lifestyle, as preached in many queer magazines, is not everything. After a liberating coming out, a good deal of sexual experience perhaps, finding a lover, celebrating at wild parties and marching in parades for gay rights, they reach a point where they wonder what the next step might be.

Where are we now? – What do we live from?

Coming in invites gays and lesbians to turn inwards after their personal experience of coming out with its obvious outward orientation. This turning within helps one give shape to one's life. Coming in touches the deepest layers of being: crucial life steps are taken and an advanced process of maturation follows.

I want to explore this approach further by referring to the great American spiritual master Thomas Merton (1915–1968). In this incorporation of Merton's thoughts I have been deeply touched and influenced by an unpublished text which Rev. Patrick W. Collins, PhD, kindly gave me to read and use: *From Illusions Toward Truth: Thomas Merton's 'True Self' and Gay Spirituality*. I am very thankful for this invaluable and unusual paper and I am deeply indebted to Patrick Collins for giving me new insights which I share here.

The writings of Thomas Merton reflect a personal and intense quest for authentic truth in his own life. Merton himself was always in search of his true self. For Merton, all spirituality is a quest to become as fully human as possible, to express oneself completely in one's lifetime. It means living more and more out of the Higher or True Self. We are moving towards a complete integration of the Higher Self, which is the divine in each person.

Merton wrote:

> *To be holy is a question of appreciating where one is in life and learning to foster the vital connections that are already operative. [...] I must therefore know myself, and know both the good and the evil that are in me. It will not do to know only one and not the other: only the good, or only the evil. I must then be able to live the life God has given me, living it fully and fruitfully, and making good use even of the evil that is in it. To live well myself is my first and essential contribution to the well-being of all mankind and to the fulfilment of man's collective destiny. To live well means for me to know and appreciate something of the secret, the mystery in myself; that which is incommunicable, which is at once myself and not myself, at once in me and above me.*

(Conjectures of a Guilty Bystander, p.95, quoted in Collins p.4)

Despite the diversity of the queer community, all gay and lesbian people who wish to grow spiritually must experience a coming in, or – to put it another way – must experience a kind of inner coming out to oneself, to others and to God. In other words, the journey of coming in to one's true identity, which is admittedly often difficult. Why? Collins writes:

> *Because gay people begin their journeys toward self-iden-tity and self-affirmation several steps behind others in our culture. Heterosexuals at least think they understand their orientation and identity. Straight reality is assumed to be 'normal' by the culture, the churches and even some gay people. Everyone is presumed to be heterosexual. Gays are abnormal, at least statistically, and even are described by some religious traditions as 'intrinsically disordered' and 'an abomination'. Yet through history, a small minority have always been same-sex-oriented – and often these have been some of the most creative and spiritually aware lead-ers in every age. But their gifts usually have not been understood as coming from their full human identity,*

including their sexual orientation as a major energy for their love and creativity. Usually this has been either unknown, denied or dismissed.

(Collins pp.4,5)

I agree with Collins when he says that the soul is the core of one's self which needs to be extracted from all of one's psychic modalities (thinking, wishing, feeling, remembering, imagining and sexual orientation) in order to free it to infuse those various modalities, rather than those modalities themselves becoming the ultimate basis of personal identity. These are mere descriptions of the self, not the real self. To make part of oneself the magnet for the whole of oneself is what Merton calls living out of the false self – which includes only partial self and partial truth. The truth of one's identity is larger than any single modality and description. Indeed it is more than all of the modalities combined.

In Psychosynthesis there is a very helpful model of 'subpersonalities'. We take on different roles and aspects in our lives, such as our profession, the lover, the partner, the fearful one, the daredevil, etc. The danger lies in the trap of over-identifying with one or more of our subpersonalities. This is the problem that occurs when we identify only with our homosexuality. As with all subpersonalities, in the end it is important to break through and live from the Higher Self, as Roberto Assagioli (the founder of Psychosynthesis) called it, or from the True Self, the term Thomas Merton used.

The Higher Self is the place where God is present. (This is the True Self, the God-ness, existing within the socially constructed and self-constructed ego self.) We become what we are – in Merton's words:

At the centre of our being is a point of nothingness which is untouched by sin and by illusion, a point of pure truth, a point or spark which belongs entirely to God, which is never at our disposal, from which God disposes of our lives, which is inaccessible to the fantasies of our own mind or the brutalities of our own will. This little point of nothingness and of absolute poverty is the pure glory of God in us.

(Conjectures of a Guilty Bystander, p.142, quoted in Collins p.6)

I agree with Collins that in Christian terms it is the self found 'in Christ' in which Spirit merges and meshes with spirit. It is the person St Paul speaks of when he says: 'There is neither Jew nor Greek, woman nor man, slave nor free. All are one in Christ Jesus.' (Galatians 3:28) One might add to Paul's pairs of opposites that there is 'neither gay nor straight, married nor single'. In Christ all are whole and all are one.

This growth from self-hatred toward self-appreciation is what can happen when one comes out from hiding one's true sexual orientation from oneself, from others and from God. Those who have successfully come out 'feel themselves full of something that they have never experienced before: a sense of power. That power is caused, in part, by freeing the energy that we have previously been using to deny and disguise ourselves.' (Collins p.6) Gay men and lesbian women may then be ready to begin the journey toward their unique identity, their True Self. For all persons in every age, embarking on this journey with intentionality and passion is what it means to become authentic, whole and holy.

From lie to authentic life

Those who have read some of Thomas Merton's books will agree that the issue of journeying from falseness and hiding towards an authentic life was of paramount importance for him:

For me to become a saint means to be myself. Therefore the problem of sanctity and salvation is in fact the problem of finding out who I am and of discovering my true self. [...] God leaves us free to become whatever we like. We can be ourselves or not, as we please. We are at liberty to be real, or to be unreal. We may be true or false, the choice is ours. [...] Causes have effects, and if we lie to ourselves and to others, then we cannot expect to find truth and reality

*whenever we happen to want them. If we have chosen the
way of falsity we must not be surprised that truth eludes us
when we finally come to need it. We are called to share with
God in creating our true identity.*

(New Seeds of Contemplation pp.31-32, quoted in Collins p.7)

Collins makes it a central point in his text that honesty is the
path. What might this call toward the True Self mean for the individual spiritual journeys of gay people? A mystic spirituality for
gays and lesbians must help them open up to understanding and
experiencing their own inner reality, and they must come to see
their innate attractions and loves as a blessing rather than a
curse. Many gay men and lesbian women are forced to live clos-
eted, unauthentic lives by both their own internalised homophobia and the external homophobia which permeates their culture
and the churches. Such self-hatred poisons the journey toward
being one's own unique reflection of the image and likeness of
God. In this way people may lack the inner and outer freedom to
create their true identity with God. This 'falseness' is not unique
to those oriented toward their own sex. Merton wrote: 'Every one
of us is shadowed by an illusory person; a false self.' (*New Seeds
of Contemplation* p.34, quoted in Collins p.7) He believed that we
come to realise that true identity is not what appears on the
surface. Who we really are is not the mask we wear or the role
imposed by our upbringing and our society. No, we are much
more than that. In fact, much of what is on the surface is not
truly us at all.

This is a sound spiritual insight for gay persons. It encourages us to leave the closet of imposed deceptions and roles, the
masks of the false self that have been created by heterosexist
and homophobic definitions and expectations. But some queer
people all too readily become trapped in another closet, this
one constructed by gays and lesbians themselves – namely, and
principally in my view, the gay male subculture. This becomes
the 'second closet' as Collins calls it. This new closet can be
either extreme promiscuity, with its lack of commitment, or

materialistic consumerism. Spiritual growth for lesbian and gay persons involves moving beyond both of these closets. Collins describes this perfectly:

> *A new ghetto of prescribed places and behaviour, a new prison of images and stereotypes can replace the original closet for subculture-oriented gay persons. While there is clearly a value in safe places and joyous and comfortable sharing with like-oriented persons, there is a danger that this can become a new kind of isolation and separatism. It is one not imposed by the rejection of heterosexism but one freely chosen by same-sex-oriented persons for the sake of security and the avoidance of those engagements with heterosexuals that could stimulate mutual growth for gays and straights alike. Gay spiritualities need to be especially attuned to this second false self and its traps. Like everyone, gay persons need to transcend the cultural location of the ego personality and discover it more deeply in the soul, the True Self.*

(Collins p.7)

The journey through the desert

The story of the liberation and exodus of the Hebrew people from slavery in Egypt, and their forty-year journey to a new land, has been a shining example and model for many liberation movements. Martin Luther King used this story as a metaphor and motivating force for the liberation of black people in the USA, and many gay and lesbian leaders and writers have taken up the image of the exodus in their fight for justice and liberation.

Where are we now on our journey? I think that, even with all the success and progress for which we can be hugely thankful, we are still in the desert. After we 'moved away' from homophobic society and unshackled ourselves from heterosexist laws and norms, we encountered a new subculture. While this new place has many constructive elements, it limits lesbian women and even more so gay men, and may even commercially exploit them.

Gay theologian Richard Cleaver suggests that the movement towards liberation has been sidetracked into 'a system of commercial products and institutions. We have created a new Egypt, where we can feel as if our liberation has already been won.' (Cleaver, *Know My Name*, pp.24-25)

Paul Monette, the late gay author who died of AIDS, adds:

> *To come out is not to fully understand who we are. You have to take the energy of coming out and then you have to study ... I've come to understand in the last couple of years that being gay is about something more profound than my sexual nature, my carnal nature. This deeper core that we're calling 'gay soul' is something we have to learn from one another as we grow more human with one another.*

(Monette in Thompson, *Gay Soul*, p.23-24)

This all raises the question of whether a large part of the gay and lesbian population has been assimilated into a system of commercial values.

In many parts of the Western world there used to exist an erroneous and violent image of lesbians and more so of gay men: homosexuals as child molesters and dangerous, sick perverts. This has now been replaced by another extreme image, that of the commercial gay scene itself. Gay men are presented as gorgeous young creatures with beautiful muscular bodies; they are sexually obsessed and financially potent. While most gays have put the old homophobic lies of society behind them, and society has of course changed in itself, many gays have adopted a new image that is just as distorted as the old one.

After their coming out a large number of gays and lesbians celebrate this liberating step in their subculture or community. They openly rejoice in being different and having special gifts. But at the same time there is a conscious or unconscious quest for reference points, role models and appropriate patterns of behaviour. While things are slowly changing for the better, there are still not enough examples of how to be queer in a constructive, holistic, life-affirming way. Local gay and lesbian groups often offer an alternative to the hedonistic and material-istic scene, but there is still some way to go.

I am not the only one who considers this a problematic aspect of the queer movement. In the August 2001 issue of the national Austrian queer magazine *Pride* (pp.56–57,) three gay men write about their frustration with the gay scene – and I think it is not just the case in Austria when they write:

What's on offer in the local pubs and clubs is nearly always aimed at a young, dance-crazy public which is used to overly loud music ... For some reason unknown to me many bar-keepers in my local gay scene seem to try hard to keep people over 30 out. The gay scene in my town reminds me of a caricature of the Indian caste system, with the differ-ence that there is a clear boundary drawn between young and old.

In the brochure of the annual national gay and lesbian confer-ence in Boldern, close to Zürich, the title of the 2001 programme 'Yesterday lesbian and gay, tomorrow queer?' is followed by the comment:

In more and more movies and TV shows there is an increas-ing number of gay and lesbian characters. The relation-ships of prominent queer folk are described with relish and pleasure in the tabloid press. The designer Wolfgang Joop said in an interview that our society is being homosexu-alised and that the differences get more blurred. Every-thing goes, and society is levelled and homogenised by becoming more feminine, in a visual sense among others. Fashion is the ersatz religion, how to pose is more impor-tant then content. The heterosexual and homosexual scenes are becoming increasingly similar. Indifference towards others, hedonistic striving after pleasure, the cult of youth and profit-motivated thinking become ever more predomi-nant. But in this societal remodelling there are also oppor-

tunities that we need to take advantage of. Men and women
must search for and acknowledge these opportunities. Then
our being queer has a real chance in the future and in our
society, too.

As this brochure suggests, the gay subculture parallels the
'heterosexual scene' in many ways. There are numerous similari-
ties –sex saunas, brothels, swinger clubs and so-called massage
parlours. So the gay sex scene is nothing 'original' or specifically
gay but just a mirror of the long-established straight sex scene.
The same is true of advertisements: they may now include gay
people and be aimed at them, but, just like ads aimed at straight
people, they depend on youth and sexual attractiveness to sell us
things. The big question is: Should we as queer people be copy-
ing all that?

Even with all the growing awareness and interest in spirituality, our Western society is still too often dominated by a materialistic approach. We remain a society where performance and
achievement, youth and health, attractiveness and making
money are on top of many a list. So we have to ask a question
about how far gay subculture has taken on the imperative of
society in general and, therefore, once again has been assimilated by society, albeit on another level and in another way.

Ram Dass reflects on the wisdom of an integrated gay identity,
which is increasingly common among the maturing gay population today. He advises those who live largely in the gay
subculture to let go of models of existence and delve into the
richness of the moment.

You've reduced yourself into a shadow of who you are,
through clinging to concepts instead of understanding that
the true nature of being is not knowing you know, it's
simply being [...] There's something else going on, and real-
izing this is awakening [...] Sex and social relationship is not
enough – eventually you will be driven into spiritual awak-
ening [...] Awakening is the recognition that there are
many planes of consciousness and that you exist on them

all. You are limiting yourself incredibly to define yourself only in terms of the physical/psychological planes, as if they were absolutely real.

(Ram Dass in Thompson, *Gay Soul* pp.161,166)

Ram Dass would probably agree with Merton's related words: 'If what people want is food and sex, let them have that, and see if they can get along with that only, and without meaning. (*Conjectures of a Guilty Bystander* p.301, quoted in Collins p.8)

A central concern of all mature spirituality in all serious religious traditions in this world is that we are only free when we search for and find God in the core of our being; when we let go of the dependences and addictions of our urges and personality traits.

What to do about the falsity and illusion created first of all by heterosexist homophobia and then by the gay subculture itself? How can we avoid or come out of the second closet? Thomas Merton wrote:

The difficult ascent from falsity toward truth is accomplished not through pleasant advances in wisdom and insight, but through the painful unlayering of levels of falsehood and untruths deeply embedded in our consciousness, lies which cling more tightly than a second skin.

(Conjectures of a Guilty Bystander p.296, quoted in Collins p.8)

To add to this observation by Merton but also to look at a contrasting aspect, I want to emphasise that joyful and humorous experiences can also help us discover our truth. However, the painful side – the dark night of the soul as the Spanish mystic John of the Cross called it – is part of the process: it is like peeling away the layers of an onion – tears and all!

We are regularly confronted in our lives with limitations on our identity, with the need to wear a mask, to be untrue to parts of ourselves or to over-identify with parts of our being that control us. This can arise from our education and upbringing in society or from our wounds, power games, inferiority complexes or unconscious group constraints.

In all great religious and spiritual traditions a central focus is the letting go of the ego or false self. Of course, it is not formulated in the same way in all traditions but nevertheless the intention is the same. Many readers may be familiar with the story of Jesus and the rich young man. Jesus invites him to sell everything and give it to the poor. Or take the Gospel story of Jesus and Nicodemus, whom Jesus invites to be born again in Spirit. In the Jewish tradition we find the motif of repentance or turning around as we would say in German ('Umkehr'). Letting go of the false self is a point also made very clearly by the Eastern religions. Enlightenment in Hinduism has to do with recognising one's true identity, and a central pivot of Buddhism is letting go and leaving behind what is unreal and illusory.

How can we today accurately describe the letting go of the ego? This has been a major question for me and I have struggled to comprehend this as gay man in our times. This quest has also to do with my past: although I experienced some helpful aspects of religious education in my childhood, I also suffered religious abuse. I had to go to so-called 'child evangelisation' meetings or children's Bible classes where we pre-pubertal children were taught in words and pictures that we should remove our 'egoistic I' from the 'throne' of our heart so that the Lord Jesus could take a seat on this chair. Of course, these intrusive formulations and ignorant demands went down very badly, because as a child I did not have enough experience to distinguish between the absolutely necessary personal 'I' and what is called 'ego'. For a long time it has been clear to me that we need a strong and healthy I on a personal level in order to make decisions, to assert ourselves, to be aware of our will and to take action. We clearly must not mistake the personal I for the ego. We need our personal I to fight for our dignity and for human rights. While I do not know if this kind of 'child evangelising' still happens, I believe that some of the problems with the evangelical concept and interpretation of 'being born again' have to do with this confusion between the personal I and the ego.

To be attached to the ego means ultimately that we are not free. We are clinging to something that is unreal, something that conforms to a different law than does our true self, that forces us to assume a mask or embark on a destructive mode of living. Essentially this attachment keeps us from experiencing the depth of our being and benefiting from it. From the depth of our being we can evolve into the dimension of Christ in us and be able to hear the divine voice within ourselves.

The intention to be on a spiritual path is always fundamental to the process of leaving the ego behind, and it is important to let oneself become more and more grounded in this divine reality. We need increasingly to reflect on our decisions and priorities out of this depth of being. In this way, we will be able eventually to let go of ego, break open our destructive behaviour patterns, and discern what is illusion and lie. Of course, overcoming consumerism, hedonism and attachment has its painful side. This is because often our masks and addictions are our responses to being deeply wounded in the past.

On my personal spiritual journey to heal the religious abuse in my childhood, I have found comfort and direction by engaging critically but openly with Hinduism, Buddhism (especially Zen) and most of all the Christian mystics. Psychosynthesis has guided me to rethink and develop further my ideas about the psychological and spiritual nature of humankind.

Just as the Higher Self, as understood by Psychosynthesis, resides in the transpersonal level or the higher consciousness, the personal self or the personal I is found in the personal level or middle consciousness, where we also find the subpersonalities. The false self develops mainly through societal and group conditioning – whether through education, being hurt, traumatic experiences, identifying with one's urges rather than with one's True Self. And that false identity is where the process of change, letting go and healing must start. At the same time we need to acknowledge our relationship with the Higher Self and fundamentally trust this True Self. This process is related to 'repentance'. For me it was very helpful to consider this process in psychological terms, because the religious words were so emotionally loaded.

Therefore, as gays and lesbians too we can break through to this deepest reality and live in infinite freedom and trust. We cannot truly deal with our false self by denial, ignorance or control. We are as ill as our hidden secrets. We have to name our demons so that salvation and holiness can grow in us. We have to acknowledge our dark side. This is all-important because in accepting it honestly as part of us we mitigate its power over us. This helps us to allow our True Self to express itself continuously in our life. By encountering the presence of God within us, we become healed of the fracture, the parting, between the false self and our True Self.

The realisation of our own true identity means that we are transformed by God's inner presence in such a way that we live in God, and love all of creation as God does. Although there is a lot of hard work involved in this process, in the end it is not our own work but rather God's work in us. This is what I call grace – travelling the path of Christ (Chapter 9).

There is perhaps another pain that queer people have to confront in order to be able to come in after a coming out.

Jeff Leeds, a former Jesuit, expresses this journey from exile for gay men:

> *I desire to become a liberator beckoning not only myself but others from their place of exile. In my desire to embrace this truth I have come to realise why I have spent a lifetime running from myself. I ran from place to place and from job to job never knowing the motivating force behind my restlessness and search for peace. I thought I was searching for success, and instead I was searching for myself. I needed to look no further than my heart, for it was there that I found the key to what I had been yearning a lifetime to find [...] It is to that horizon that I long to traverse and reach out to embrace.*

(Leeds in *White Crane Newsletter*, Fall 97, p.7)

We are called to reach out and embrace the True Self. But we cannot do this alone. Spiritual companioning is essential at this stage in the inner and outer liberation of gay people. This is particularly true because of the double closet and the trap of illusion. Susan Rakoczy describes such spiritual sharing as

> ... *a privileged meeting of hearts. Built on trust in the bond of the Spirit of God, two persons come together in faith to hear the story of the workings of the Spirit in the life of one of them. For the person who shares her or his experience of God, there is always the moment of 'stepping out on the water' as one begins to speak of what is most sacred in life. The listener, who is companion on the journey, is called to receive that sharing in trust and love, with encouragement and support, and, at times, with the invitation to further growth, even at the cost of pain and suffering.*

(Rakoczy, *Common Journey, Different Path* p.9)

It is not a matter of achieving some impossible and superhuman saint-like state but, as John Eudes Bamberger, writing about Thomas Merton expressed it, 'The perfect man is the man who is ever moving forward, deeper into the mystery of God...each fulfilment contains in itself the impulse to further exploration.' (Patrick Hart, ed., *Thomas Merton Monk* p.54) To be whole, to find the True Self, means to navigate through the confusing, complex wilderness of false images of oneself and of the world. On this spiritual journey with its joyful and painful aspects, with its rich experiences, we bring together the separated worlds within us. This process leads us to an encounter with purpose and joy in the depth of our being.

Coming in as being blessed

The fact that we are examining these dark and difficult sides of our lives shouldn't be misinterpreted as a need to focus on sin, evil and everything negative. This is particularly important since gays and lesbians have always been seen primarily as wicked sinners, and an overwhelming fixation on sin has been a weakness of the Christian churches through the centuries. The church has constantly overstated and distorted the sinfulness of human beings – which is actually an abuse of the church's power, designed to demean and subjugate people and make them overly dependent. And, as we all know, the area of sexuality has been especially singled out. Sadly, today's conservative evangelicals and traditionalist Catholics who fight against gay and lesbian people have not yet learnt this lesson.

As Matthew Fox, with his creation spirituality, and other theologians have shown, we need to rediscover God's blessing. All human beings, including LGB people, go through a journey of estrangement and need to experience reconciliation and salvation, but we are all blessed beings to begin with. Coming in has therefore also to do with joy that leads to an explicit and spontaneous 'joie de vivre'. The one who has reconciled himself or herself experiences deep joy. Furthermore, we gain a holistic and harmonious insight into our sexuality through this process of coming in. And rejoicing in what we are includes an appreciation of all creation.

Coming in calls us to a new creative ethic – to make decisions concerning partnership and sexuality based neither, on the one hand, on moralising and homophobia nor, on the other hand, on hedonism and the behaviour of the majority. It means making decisions out of a liberated spirit, out of the Higher Self, in connection with Christ in us. This deep integration and grounding allows me to get in touch with my dignity and that of my fellow human beings. In discussion with other people who are on 'the road less travelled' as Scott Peck called it, I have time to practise and to grow. I live my sexuality with self-esteem. I look into the eyes of my beloved partner.

Coming in to the source of life

Of course, coming out and coming in are not neatly separated. Some gays and lesbians go through an important initial spiritual process that leads to their coming out. Coming out may therefore have a sacramental character; in itself it is a great step toward spiritual integrity. But I feel it is important to make clear that the process of development does not end with coming out. We have not reached the goal of our journey as queer people. We have not attained the 'happy ending'. On the contrary: now our life process can move into a new dimension and our spiritual growth accelerate.

Coming in invites us to pause for a moment, to trust and to allow God's spirit in to lead and inform us. Coming in calls for 'instruments' for playing its symphony of life: daily meditation, regular prayer, spiritual ritual, lively worship services, celebrating open religious communities, awe in nature, involvement in the arts. These are essential tools for spiritual growth and for finding our way through our false self to our True Self.

I end this chapter again with the image of a water source, a spring. Maybe you have seen such a spring in nature, where water first splashes out of the earth. I deem it a powerful, life-giving image that nourishes and inspires the imagination.

Coming in means nakedness – freedom from prejudice, role-play, assumptions, masks and lies. Through the fire of God's spirit the wax of your personality will be formed. You are naked before God, the source of all life. Look at yourself in the beauty of your being, in the clear water of your soul. Delve, dive deep into the spring. To find that spring, that original source, your thirst is your signpost.

I am touched by the aforementioned story of the Samaritan woman at the well (John 4:1–14). If you read the whole story, you realise that this woman so far has always directed her aims and desires externally – be it in relationships with men or in outer forms of religion. Jesus breaks through this pattern and changes her perspective. 'Whoever drinks the water I give will never be thirsty again. The water that I give will always be a spring welling up to give eternal life.'

Coming in is the process of getting in touch with this inner spring, this well of spirit, and drawing from one's own depth the water of life. It is living from this indwelling Self and allowing oneself and the world to transform.

Let the last words of this chapter be a personal prayer experience:

Christ says: Coming in invites you on a journey into your depth in order to expand your consciousness. Discover the water of the Spirit. The well is in you. Find peace in me. My gates are wide open, for gays and lesbians and for everyone.

QUESTIONS

Are you involved in a process of coming in right now in your life? How could you start or deepen it?

Which parts of the mainstream gay and lesbian movement are you thankful for?

Do you feel that you are too much caught up in the over-commercialised or destructive aspect of the gay scene? If yes, what does that mean in practical terms and how could you liberate yourself from it?

What does it mean in your present life situation to let go of the ego and possibly destructive life patterns, and therefore to allow your life to be guided by Christ in you? (Or whatever term you would use according to your own spiritual background or psychological framework – for example, your True Self or Higher Self, the divine ground of your being, etc.)

SUGGESTIONS

Reflect on the areas of your personality and life where you are still imprisoned, overpowered, influenced in a negative way: be it by the church, heterosexual society, male/female role expectations, gay subculture or the lesbian scene or whatever.

Sign up for a weekend or week-long course of contemplation. Look for a local meditation group. Or, as I learnt from some gay Jesuits, the exercises of Ignatius of Loyola can also be helpful for the coming in process.

Write on a large piece of paper 'Coming Out' and on another piece 'Coming In'. Do a brainstorm and spontaneously write down whatever comes into your head as you reflect on your life.

EXERCISE

A short introduction to contemplation

As you may be aware, meditation practices have become more and more popular in the West during the last twenty or thirty years. Meditation has also become an important tool for many Christians and a way of prayer. For me, one of the big hopes is that the transformation of consciousness will accelerate, because it is essential for the survival of the planet as well as for resolving all the human crises that humanity has brought about.

Contemplation is a form of meditation. While the content and intention of this kind of meditation has a long tradition in the Western world, the methodology, as taught in most contemplation wokshops and classes today, is derived from the Japanese Zen tradition.

All forms of meditation attempt to touch a deeper level of human consciousness, thereby helping us to become grounded and centred; or as Christians to open ourselves up to the Christ within: or, as others would say, to experience unity with God, the core or ground of our being.

I started practising contemplation over 15 years ago. Since then it has not only become a favourite practice of my own but has also became a central focus in the spirituality of our Community and order. Along with many others I use the word contemplation to describe a form of meditation in a Christian context – although, as mentioned above, the outward form of the practice is derived from Zen.

It is clear that coming in silence before God and letting go of all that distracts us is not a new invention. You only need to look at some of the writings of the mystics like John of the Cross, Theresa of Avila, etc., to be convinced of this. The gift of Zen to Christians and other people in the West is that it gives us a structure that has been tried and tested for centuries. It is a treasury of experience. So the timing, the way we sit, the breathing, and some of the ritual has been inspired by Zen.

We do this in full awareness that the emptiness, the void that opens up within us can be trusted and accepted. Moreover, we trust that Christ is in us. Others of you would describe this differently, according to your own particular background. I cannot say what is going to happen if you commit yourself to a regular practice of contemplation. Some of you will experience little change, while others will undergo shorter or longer periods of deep connectedness with the core of being.

Over the years I have had various deep experiences, often during contemplation weeks. These are, of course, more intense than normal daily practice, with up to six or seven hours of sitting during the course of one day. During such sessions I have had to deal with physical pain and to accept it. Another thing that can happen, and is something that I have experienced, is that emotional pain surfaces, perhaps in the form of memories. While it may be helpful to talk about this with the leader afterwards, during the session itself it is important to accept the experience and to let it go. For me this was a healing process. On other occasions, I entered a much deeper level of consciousness, unbounded by time and space. In these moments I felt at one with God and with creation, where the boundaries of the ego melted away. (This is difficult to describe in words, because you can only talk about it after the experience is over.) It is not something that can be understood in a purely academic sense, but rather has to be experienced. What we can realistically expect is that we will be able to centre and to experience a cleansing process of the soul.

In contemplation we let go of whatever keeps our mind busy or distracts us: thoughts, fantasies, images, dreams, etc. It is important not to judge ourselves whenever we find we have wandered off mentally in this way. We lovingly accept whatever comes up and let it go again immediately. A big help in this is our breathing. We breathe regularly to our own rhythm. If we find we have been distracted, we can always return to our breath. We trust that the emptiness that opens up in us is not a yawning abyss but that in our deepest core it is Christ who is waiting for us.

Put a watch on the floor or set an alarm clock that isn't too loud. Start with ten minutes. If you practise regularly, you may eventually extend the session up to half an hour. Ideally use a special meditation-timer which uses a flash of light rather than a sound to mark the elapsed time.

Sit on a chair or meditation cushion, if possible about half a metre distant from a wall. Sit upright in a good posture. Let your shoulders relax. Hold your head erect. Keep your eyes slightly open and focused on a point on the floor between one and three metres away from you. Rest your left hand on top of your right, palms up, and let the thumbs touch each other.

As far as possible, keep your body silent and serene. Try to refrain from moving or scratching – although you can of course use your handker-chief if you sneeze! If you find yourself unable to sit through the whole ten minutes – for example, if you start feeling dizzy – please feel free to leave the room in silence without disturbing other meditators.

You can repeat this exercise every day and increase the time up to twenty minutes or to an upper limit of thirty minutes. If you want to learn more about the background of contemplation there is plenty of literature available, or even better attend a course in contemplation or in Zen at a retreat centre.

Of course, there are also other forms of meditation. There is a kind of meditation where you use a mantra which you repeat silently and constantly during the session, such as 'Christ' or 'Lord Jesus, have mercy upon me' or similar words or phrases. There is a widespread Christian meditation movement founded by John Main and of course there are other meditation traditions originating within the Hindu or Buddhist faiths. Some of these also use mantras. In addition, spiritual teachers like Andrew Cohen have opened up meditation centres around the world.

PRAYER

God,
I thank You for the movement of coming out and coming in.
These holy energies sustain my life and foster evolution.
I let go of all that holds me back and blocks me.
I surrender myself into Your hands.

Nine

The Way of Christ
for Gays and Lesbians

In this chapter I take the opportunity to interpret the different stages of the life of Jesus Christ and apply them to the context of today's gays and lesbians. The various stages of the way of Christ can become a reality and a spur to spiritual development in the life of homosexual men and women. They encourage and inspire us to set out on the path leading to liberation, spiritual growth and creativity, a journey that opens us up to the whole spectrum of human experience: joy and sadness, fear and courage, life and death.

What do I mean by 'the way of Christ'? Jesus of Nazareth followed a unique path: he lived a one-of-a-kind life, which ultimately moved – and still moves – the entire world. Certainly, by the time of his baptism Jesus had recognised and experienced himself as the 'Christ', the 'Son of God'. This is clearly exemplified in his words: 'The Father and I are one.'

For this life journey of the historical Jesus we have only biblical evidence. The writers of the gospels, in choosing and editing previously word-of-mouth accounts of the life of Jesus, were even at this early stage filtering and conceptualising the various aspects of the story. This process was further influenced by the fact that they were writing for a very specific audience – believers in Christ who were living at that time. Throughout the centuries the mystics in particular have lived and interpreted the stages of Jesus's life as the basis and explanation of their own spiritual and life experiences. They have made themselves familiar with the stages of this way and up to a point have identified with the life of Jesus. This is, for them, a constant source of strength and they experience the presence of Christ as a reality: 'I am with you till the end of the world ...'

This path cannot be perceived either as a straight line or as a closed circle. We have rather to imagine it as an ascending spiral. Every time the spiral rises a full turn, all the stages are reiterated. So we may experience the five stages over and over again during our life but each time we are able to respond in a more mature and highly evolved way. Each new stage integrates the experiences of the previous stage. Pierre and Catherine Brunner-

Dubey write in *Kraftvoll Einkehren* about this path:

> *The way of Christ revolves in the form of a spiral; the Christ, the Alpha and Omega, the absolute awareness, the everlasting reality, the perfect love, which is constant in everything that is born and decays, perfect among all its imperfection. This way changes our lives by bringer closer the experience of Christ's reality. It leads us deeper into Christ's mystery and by the power of his drawing closer raises us step by step into the realm of the divine.*
>
> (p.151)

To expand further on the image of the spiral, it means for example that we do not go through the stage of resurrection only once and then leave this chapter behind for the rest of our life. Not at all. These steps are not unique in the sense that, once taken, they become something completed and in the past. Of course, we come to this earth by means of physical birth literally only once and through corporal death we depart from it only once. But during our life we continually experience processes of dying, and when a new stage of spiritual growth awaits, the Holy Spirit invites us to be born again. I must stress, though, that this pattern of life, this path of spiritual development, does not call into question the uniqueness of the personal path of Jesus and as a consequence it does not imply, for example, that we are all called to become martyrs. The essential point is that our own experiences of suffering and dying, which we encounter in various dimensions, can be understood in the light of Jesus's suffering on the cross. This provides us with a strong sense of support and solidarity at difficult times of our lives.

The stages of the way of Christ are: Birth – Baptism – Vocation – Cross – Resurrection. Within each of theses five stages there is a gift for us, a message, a resource that enables us to work through the challenges of life. This path calls us to enter into a process of growth or transformation and thereby it liberates us.

I want to take you now on a walk through those different life stages and to examine them from a gay and lesbian perspective.

1. Birth/Becoming Human/Incarnation
You are created and wanted

You will note that in the description of the birth of Jesus in the Bible a big issue is made of the fact that this event is desired by God in every respect. It is not cast into doubt by the unpleasant aspects surrounding the birth, such as the homelessness of Mary and Joseph. The famous stable was an emergency shelter that had nothing to do with the romanticism and cosiness of most of today's nativity plays. But all these difficult circumstances do not call into question the good will of God towards this child. Later, the family has to escape overnight to prevent the murder of their baby. Jesus and his parents become refugees and seek asylum in Egypt.

As is true for many heterosexuals for different reasons, we as homosexual men and women are often born into circumstances that are not favourable. But there is one main difference that distinguishes us: even with all the increasing tolerance and support in Western society and other places, it would be hard to find parents who expect or certainly hope that their child will turn out gay or lesbian. Consciously or unconsciously, almost everybody expects their child to be heterosexual. This can be seen clearly in the education process at home and at school. Children who grow up in conservative environments receive the message, perhaps between the lines but nevertheless loud and clear, that being gay or lesbian is undesirable or even an abomination. While in countries with strong racist tendencies the children of the victimised group know the example and the solidarity of other children and adults of their kind, most gays and lesbian grow up feeling alone and isolated. Jesus was in his own way different and considered 'queer' as a result of his self-awareness, his message and lifestyle, and how he understood his calling,. This caused him a great deal of trouble, especially from the religious fundamentalists of his time. They despised aspects of his lifestyle (such as his healing mission and his friendship with outcasts) and considered his teaching 'unbiblical' – contrary to the laws laid down in their standard religious texts.

This is an important connection for gays and lesbians, today's queer people. It is essential to become aware on every level – spiritual, emotional and intellectual – that God wants us, complete with our sexual orientation. If you are a member of a trusted group it might be a helpful and challenging suggestion to affirm it out loud within the group: I am created and wanted by God with my sexuality.

2. Baptism/Birth of a new consciousness
You are my beloved son, my beloved daughter; on you my favour rests

We know little about the first thirty years of Jesus's life. Did he ever have a lover? Was he celibate all his life? Or was he perhaps even married? Due to the circumstances of that time and the non-biographical intention of the authors of the New Testament we know nothing of his sexual orientation. But around the age of thirty Jesus had his spiritual coming out. His new spiritual awareness was activated in the context of a ritual of baptism. As a symbolic act John the Baptist ceremonially immersed him in water and fulfilled the role of a ritual master for Jesus's birth into a new consciousness. As a result Christ recognises who he is. He hears a voice: 'You are my beloved son; on you my favour rests.' It is right and with good reason that the Christian tradition emphasises the fact that, in Jesus, God became human in a unique and total act of solidarity. But this experience of being a child of God, this new awareness, is not limited to Jesus. Jesus himself makes it clear over and over again that our awareness of our relationship with God can and must be radically transformed. He invites us to see that relationship no longer as slaves, but as mature sons and daughters of God. This totally alters our relationship with our environment in all its dimensions and it profoundly changes our understanding of faith. The core of God is now experienced as love. So the central point that Jesus made was that our awareness must be transformed. We must be born again spiritually. We realise that we are children of God and live accordingly.

This self-awareness is fundamentally important for a healthy spiritual life as gays and lesbians. As a by-product it creates a new basis for dialogue with church-oriented people. As lesbian and gay people, we are loved by the divine reality. God our father and our mother has put his/her favour on us. This is the starting point for a mature spiritual journey.

If we translate the expression 'sons and daughters' radically into the wider context, it has major consequences. All human beings are our brothers and sisters, even if they themselves cannot or do not want to see it that way. This fosters among other things a profound shift in the way we deal with the dignitaries of church institutions. As brothers and sisters, they are at the same level as we are. Therefore we need not be distracted by projections of parental authority – or even play the parental game at all. Even the 'holy father' in Rome is none other than our brother!

I presume that a majority of the readers of this book have been baptised as infants. At that age we had no say in that decision. It obviously had no connection with the various aspects of our life today, including our sexual orientation. In some parts of the world with a Christian background, especially in Europe, the number of people who have never been baptised is constantly growing. For those who are gay and lesbian this development may have a happy side: their reality as gay and lesbian adults could be included in a ritual of baptism. An adult baptism is a celebration of a new awareness of being a child of God, of being created by God as a unique being, and affirming the willingness to live out of this consciousness. For those of us who have already been baptised, a new ritual could be created to affirm and celebrate being a gay son, a lesbian daughter of God.

I myself was baptised as an infant. In my case I included this aspect of awareness in a ceremony of blessing with my partner in 1988. (I describe this service in the chapter on partnership.) Services such as these offer a further opportunity to address the issue of our awareness.

3. Vocation/Calling/Task
Go your own way of unfolding, surrender and service

After his baptism Jesus recognised his vocation. The change of consciousness bore fruit, without which it would not have been a real change. Jesus came to understand his mission, which was to teach and to live the good news of love, liberation and salvation. He was aware of the greatness and complexity of his task and he knew that he could not separate teaching from acting. The word was to be lived.

Through the years I have met, accompanied, counselled and befriended many people. Regardless of their sexual preferences I have noted their profound indecisiveness and confusion when it comes to the question of life direction and personal vocation. The reasons are various – psychological, social and sociological. Although this is not the place to go into this complex issue, I think it is an important one to address in our lives.

In this book I am particularly concerned about our vocation in regard to being gay or lesbian. Of course, this concern has not only an individual aspect but also a social one. Besides all the personal issues that influence our decisions in this area, our calling and task will be at least partly determined by the situation of the world. So the process of searching for our vocation needs to take account of some questions beyond our personal life situation and desires. What does humanity need at this time of global crisis? Where will my talents make the most difference? How does the state of the planet, and my priorities in relation to that, affect my choices of profession and partner?

There are some tools available that provide help and support in personal growth and unfoldment, deepening of consciousness and stronger awareness of potential and vocation. For example, I am thinking of the different forms of meditation. Roberto Assagioli and other transpersonal teachers call it the main road to a creative broadening and change of consciousness. Whatever form of meditation is used (Zen, contemplation, etc.), it is something that needs regular and long-term practice. Also of paramount importance is a mentor. This may be a spiritual director or a counsellor or therapist with an understanding of the transpersonal dimension. Of course, it needs to be someone who is either homosexual or who has a serious positive concern for and acceptance of gays and lesbians and their specific issues. We need an environment of respect in order to open up and to grow.

4. The Cross/Dying/Letting Go
Suffering as experience on the road of liberation

The story continues: Jesus gets into big trouble. His radical lifestyle, his liberating good news, his solidarity in friendship with despised outsiders and his consciousness of being the Son of God do not ride well with the establishment of his time. He makes people angry, and experiences hostility, threats and violence which ultimately lead to a cruel execution on the cross. The religious fundamentalist teachers in particular become Jesus's major enemies. But Jesus has the courage to live his life out and continues on his way, despite his fear of the suffering to come. He experiences a frightening moment of deep agony and isolation on the cross: 'My God, my God, why have you forsaken me?'

All human beings suffer. And we all have to die and leave this world. We suffer as a result of illness or because of the death of those we love. Even today fighting for justice can lead to consequences that cause us suffering. Throughout history gays and lesbians have experienced discrimination, oppression, torture and persecution – and they still do in certain parts of the world, even at the beginning of the 21st century. In about fifty per cent of countries today, same-sex love is still forbidden by law and is punished by harsh social exclusion or imprisonment. In nations such as Iran or Saudi-Arabia, where Islamic extremists are in control, this includes whipping or the death penalty. In the Western world, on the other hand, there is still, sadly, a disproportionate number of gay and bisexual men affected by AIDS.

I too have known periods of suffering due to my being gay or because of my commitment to justice for gay and lesbian people. As I describe in more detail in the chapter 'Wounded Healers', at the age of 23 I had to leave a theological seminary after two years because I was gay. I was deeply hurt, almost destitute, and totally confused about my professional future. Whilst there is still much homophobia in secular society in many parts of the world, I particularly notice the violence of religious fundamentalists (most often from the Christian and Muslim traditions) against homosexual people. Whenever I hear news of that kind I feel very angered as a gay man. There are several methods I use to deal with this anger in a constructive and psychologically healthy way. One is to remember the stage in Jesus's life when he was persecuted and had to suffer. In my deepest heart I feel moved by Christ's solidarity, almost as if he were saying to me: 'I had similar experiences as you, my gay and lesbian people, have had. I too was confronted with the religious fundamentalists of my time who spoke out against me and wanted to do me harm. Being true to God and to myself led me eventually to the cross. I am with you and your anger and your pain. Continue faithfully on your journey, wherever it leads you. I am there.'

I was deeply moved by the Canadian movie *Jesus of Montreal* which follows the experiences of a group of actors staging an open-air passion play. The play has a profound and growing influence on the actors and on their lives. This has nothing to do with the glorification of suffering. It's about the difficult task of accepting the dark and painful sides of our lives. I don't know if I will live long enough to see an end to the hate-filled tirades of US 'evangelists' towards gays and lesbians, or the neo-Nazi threats against homosexuals in Germany, or the execution in the name of 'Islam' of men in Saudi-Arabia for having same-sex intercourse. I have no guarantee that I will never again experience discrimination during the second part of my life. But, in all of what is going on or what awaits in the future, I feel carried and nourished by the reality of Christ in me who connects me with Jesus of Nazareth who suffered for justice.

I also want to address a different but very important aspect – that of dying. I am talking about the letting go of destructive life-patterns that block further progress towards being who one truly is. Depending on the individual's life situation the process of coming out may also include this parallel process of dying. In effect it means giving up the old image and the expectation of the outside world that we should be heterosexual. During this process it is possible that one or more people who called themselves 'friends' will leave us.

There are other areas of life too where this dying, this letting go, may be needed. One is relationships where both sides try to destroy each other. Or maybe you live your sexuality in a way that alienates and debases both you yourself and the other persons involved. In all such cases there is an opportunity to let the old you die so that there is space for a new life and new possibilities. It's time for coming in.

5. Resurrection/Transformation/Metamorphosis
Rejoice! A new beginning

The cross was not final. According to the witness of Jesus's disciples, his passing on the cross was not the end of his journey. At first it may have looked like the death of a prophet who failed in his mission and who might be forgotten sooner or later. But it turned out to be something very different. His suffering was transformative and a necessary stage in a life that would drastically alter the whole world. Some theologians emphasise that for them the resurrection and ascension have to be interpreted as symbols, as metaphors. I personally have no difficulty in believing that a unique metamorphosis of the body and a spiritualisation of matter actually occurred. It might possibly have been a glimpse of humanity's future evolution into a totally new relationship between matter and spirit. In fact, some of the great spiritual thinkers about evolution refer to this – for example, Pierre Teilhard de Chardin, who wrote from a Christian perspective, and Sri Aurobindo, who wrote from a Hindu perspective.

The way of Christ is rooted in the firm faith that death is not the final word. On a practical level, this encourages me to keep hope alive amidst circumstances in my life where I experience suffering. It allows me to have faith that transformation and a new beginning are possible. For a period in the course of my job I had contact with people with AIDS. It was important to me that I didn't have to explain their suffering but I had to accept it and be close to them, whether I could alleviate it a little or not at all. But it was also vital for me to feel in my heart that corporal death is not the end of life. I have been close to young people several times just before their death. I can't explain this in any logical way but intuitively I know that the being of these women and men lives on. For me these experiences add a personal dimension to what is written in the New Testament about our living on after corporal death.

It is useful and legitimate to apply Latin American liberation theology and some aspects of feminist theology to the situation of homosexuals. The resurrection is central to these theologies. Through suffering we move towards life. Here also the story of the exodus comes in. The way out of slavery to liberty of the Israelites in the Old Testament is an image that constantly moves us and has inspired many, like Martin Luther King in his march to freedom.

In resurrection there is a second birth. The spiral of the way of Christ completes one turn.

During the years that I have tried to live this way of Christ, all its stages have been empowering to me. The way of Christ can also be deepened through ritual, an example of which I include at the end of this chapter. It is a ritual that can be used privately or in groups during retreats. I have used it several times in worship services to great effect.

QUESTIONS

Which personal experiences in life do you associate with birth, baptism, vocation, the cross and resurrection?

Where and how did your being gay or lesbian encourage and foster you on this journey?

SUGGESTIONS

On a large piece of paper draw a circle and write down the five stages at appropriate points on the circle. Open your heart and consider which events in your life can be attributed to each of those stages.

Buy an icon of Christ – one that attracts and inspires you. In my favourite icon, a copy of an old one from the Orthodox tradition, Christ is depicted together with a young man, an apostle; the two men are holding each other and looking in the same direction. Meditate in front of this chosen icon.

EXERCISE

Meditation in movement on the way of Christ

- Rearrange the furniture in the room so that you have enough space to move around in the centre of it.
- In the centre of the room place a thick candle on a fireproof base and light it. The candle serves as a symbol of Christ, the centre around which you revolve on your way.
- Now start the meditation in movement on the way of Christ. Keeping at a distance of about a metre from the candle, walk around it, stopping five times. The first stop is also the fifth, so that at the end of your circle you are back at the first station.
- You may want to close your eyes when you stop at a station in order to go deeper inside yourself.
- Remembering to stay about one metre distant from the candle, begin with the first stage of life.

1st stage: Becoming human, Recognising oneself

- Become aware of yourself as a precious individual, a valued man or woman.
- Observe your physicality, your sexuality.
- Become aware that you have been created, with your sexual orientation, by God as he intended you to be.
- You are a woman/man of many talents. Visualise your abilities, experience your feelings, and listen to your desires, aspirations and needs.
- Observe yourself as an individual, as you are now.

2nd stage: Baptism

- In the moment that you experience yourself as a human being at your deepest level, that is the instant at which God speaks to you as he spoke to Jesus when he was baptised:
- God tells you: 'You are my beloved daughter/son; on you my favour rests.'
- Take time to take this central message in, close to your heart, and feel the unconditional love.
- Imagine God looking at you in a loving, affectionate way.
- Consider that you have been accepted as you are, right now.
- Stay for a moment with a recognition of who you are in the light of the divine.

3rd stage: Vocation, Call, Mission

- With the awareness of God's boundless love and acceptance, Jesus hears the call to live the salvation and to announce it to the world. He receives the strength to carry out this task.
- With the heartfelt knowledge that God loves you, think and feel with your intuition about where this love is taking you and how it empowers you and what your mission might be.
- Jesus said: 'I am the light of the world' (John 8:12) and 'You are the light of the world' (Matthew 5:14). Consider seriously that you, like Jesus, are already the light of the world and let this move your heart and encourage you.
- Reflect imaginatively on how the mission of living love, liberation and salvation can take shape in your present daily life and beyond.

4th stage: Dying, Letting Go, Suffering
- Jesus had to suffer on the cross. We also encounter situations that generate suffering, in particular when we decide to follow Jesus's example, to stay true to our sexual orientation and to commit ourselves to fighting towards equality and justice in this world.
- Become aware what part of your life generates suffering and feel the solidarity by being connected with Jesus.
- Jesus died on the cross. Also in our life we come to situations or turning points where it is necessary to change something. Or where it is essential that something has to die or is no longer right or life-enhancing for us. Reflect on what you want to let go of in your life and be aware that even in these challenging times someone is supporting you at every step.

5th stage: Resurrection, Metamorphosis, Transformation
- Close your eyes and imagine the loving light of the resurrected Christ shining on you from above. The light is bright, friendly and clear. It touches you, enters through the top of your head and fills every part of your body and dimension of your being.
- Feel the light, be that light. Become aware of the love, energy and hope contained in this light. Let it revitalise you and transform you through the light of the resurrected Christ.
- Now finish this exercise and slowly but surely step out of the circle so that you stand outside of it in the room.
- Open your eyes, reflect on the experience by making notes, or spend some time in prayer.

PRAYER

Christ, born to the world
Evoke in me a full and boundless Yes
to all of my life and existence.

Christ, baptised
Let me experience in the very depth of my being
that I am God's beloved daughter,
God's beloved son.

Christ, called by God
Let me unfold my potential more and more.
Let me discover and live my vocation
and give thanks and appreciation for my talents.
Let me put all of these gifts into service for the world
and all of creation.
I ask especially that my same-sex orientation
become increasingly an instrument for my growth
and therefore a contribution to the human family.

Christ, crucified
Let me experience your mystic closeness when I suffer in my life.
Help me not to silence my voice for fear of suffering.
If I encounter painful situations,
give me the courage to carry on.

Christ, resurrected
I want to trust your strength, which raises death to life.
I thank you that this strength is in me through your presence.
Let me live and act from that dimension of faith
so that with my whole heart
I shape my lifestyle as a gay man or lesbian woman
in your Holy Spirit.

Amen

Ten

Community Models
for the Spiritual Journey

In order to progress on our spiritual quest, we queer people need others with whom to share the journey. Faith is something personal but not totally private. We need each other for support, fellowship, encouragement, stimulation and challenge.

In this chapter I want to talk about different forms of spiritual community. These include exclusively gay and lesbian groups but also other models, where queer people are in the minority but are clearly appreciated, valued and respected. Of course, heterosexual people too can support us on our spiritual path. I am very grateful to Pierre and Catherine Brunner-Dubey who founded the ecumenical order to which my partner and I belong. Other people have certainly had positive experiences with heterosexual spiritual directors, facilitators of meditation courses, etc. I think that even if you decide to make your base a queer faith group, it is important to connect in other ways with heterosexual people; in this way you avoid living in a ghetto and open up opportunities for reconciliation.

In mentioning types and examples of spiritual groups for gays and lesbians, I emphasise the necessity for queer people to connect with mature lesbian women and gay men on a similar spiritual path. As you will see, the structure and intensity of possible groupings varies and serves different purposes Such groups are important in order that we can become aware of our potential and live it. All the possibilities I describe here already exist at various levels of development. At one point or another, I have had fairly extensive contact with every type of group; in the case of some of them I have been a founding member or an active participant for a period.

While here and there I touch on other religious backgrounds, my emphasis is on Christian groups. Despite the extensive homophobia that some churches still display, of all the world religions the Christian faith by far exceeds the others in terms of the number of positive books written and the groups that exist that are open to the gay and lesbian experience.

For the sake of completeness it should be mentioned that there are now gay Jewish synagogues and groups and quite a number of groups within the new age and esoteric spectrum. In Britain and North America and a few other places, there are queer Buddhist groups and centres, and good books written from this perspective are available. Gay and lesbian Indians in Britain usually meet outside a religious Hindu context but queer Muslims do connect in groups in a few Western countries like Britain and the USA, and there is an interesting project of information and reconciliation in Holland. In countries with a Muslim majority, with the possible exception of Turkey, Bosnia, Malaysia and Indonesia, gay meeting places are strongly and totally suppressed and only the internet offers the opportunity to connect. Even in the USA the national gay Muslim group keeps details of its annual conference secret for fear of violence from Islamic fundamentalists.

On the other hand, it is wonderful to discover that gay and lesbian religious groups are now definitely developing outside the so-called First and Western worlds. Queer Christian groups in particular are forming in previously unlikely places like Taiwan, China and a few African countries. Three years ago a Swiss gay friend of mine returned from spending a few years in Colombia as a representative of a Catholic Mission society. He told me that even outside the major cities, and in a country torn apart by war and terrorism, small gay and lesbian Christian groups are holding meetings. Such groups usually don't have a newsletter or a website, so they are largely invisible to the wider world, but nevertheless they exist. Of course there still is a long way to go. Richard Kirker, general secretary of LGCM, told me that he was getting many letters from gay and lesbian Christians (and a few from members of other religions too) from utterly homophobic countries in Africa and Asia, including the Arabic world, that told of their isolation and suffering. But I am convinced that gay and lesbian liberation will ultimately reach these countries, even if it takes time in some of them.

I myself have been active within the gay and lesbian Christian movement for the past quarter of a century and have started several organisations and groups in Switzerland and beyond. While living in the USA for one year and now in Britain, and through many international contacts, I have had the opportunity to see many groups at work.

I want to expand on my statement that, in addition to our own unique spiritual path, we need a 'home base', a 'being together', a spiritual context within which to grow and to serve the world. Carl Rogers, the founder of person-centred therapy, used a very simple image for the therapeutic process. Potatoes can lie for a long time in a dormant state in a cold cellar. But if you take them into a warm parlour, they start to sprout. Rogers considered this a very apt metaphor for therapy: the therapist must first of all, through an accepting and loving attitude, create a climate within which those seeking help can blossom, open up, accept themselves and change as a result.

This metaphor of the potatoes can be transferred to our own life situation: We need a personal environment that is life-affirming and therefore fosters our unfolding. More specifically, in the context of what we are discussing in this book, I think it is very important that gays and lesbians who feel called to a spiritual journey search for a group that they can connect with spiritually or that they start such support groups themselves.

I'll now outline the types of 'spiritual journey communities' that exist for queer people and give practical examples of each type. Some are almost exclusively made up of LGB folks; others are primarily heterosexual groups which offer a fully recognised place to lesbians and gays and have an inclusive language and worship tradition.

I am aware that the space I give to the description of the various organisations is uneven and subjective. This is partly because I want to highlight groups that deserve to be better known than they are. Moreover, as a member of an order, this type of community is especially close to my heart and I go into more detail about it.

a. Groups in traditional churches and denominations

This type of group may be the most common. They are usually part of an ecumenical organisation that operates nationwide like the Lesbian and Gay Christian Movement (LGCM) in Britain or the numerous denominational caucuses in the USA and other countries. Most of these organisations have local groups. I myself founded a similar ecumenical network in Switzerland in 1982. A first inspiring meeting in London with Richard Kirker in 1979 and further experiences in the USA encouraged me in this direction. The spiritual intention and practice varies from local group to local group. Some have Bible study, prayer and meditation meetings, while many others just concentrate on church-political action and socialising. Some local groups have chosen to be part of a local congregation and that is where the members get their spiritual nourishment. In Britain LGCM is a powerful instrument in challenging the homophobia of the churches and in providing local groups for individual members.

These organisations are central to bringing about positive change for gays and lesbians in the churches and many of the local groups offer support to gay and lesbian Christians – especially to those for whom affiliation with a traditional church is of great importance. Even with the Vatican still issuing severely homophobic statements from time to time, there are vital unofficial gay and lesbian Roman Catholic organisations around the world: the one in the USA is called Dignity, in Britain Quest.

It's surprising to find such queer denominational organisations even within staunchly conservative traditions. I remember that I was invited in 1987 to the national conference and retreat of 'Kinship', the gay and lesbian caucus within the Seventh-Day-Adventist Church. So practically every denomination has this kind of organisation. Even within evangelical circles in Britain and the USA there are groups made up of homosexual and heterosexual Christians who are striving to make the good news of the Gospel heard amidst the bad news spread by ignorant fundamentalists.

A further point to consider is whether these organisations also offer retreats. LGCM for example offers a big one-week retreat every other year. I was asked to lead such a retreat in 2004 together with Rev. Cass Howes. It was a great experience for all involved, and I trust that many impulses flowed into the regional groups as a result. It's important for such organisations not to become so overwhelmed by their mission to fight for justice and full inclusion in the Christian denominations that they forget the spiritual hunger of their members.

When trying out this type of organisation, or more importantly its local group, do check how much spiritual nourishment it offers. I know from my experience with such groups on the European continent that many are not built on a deep spiritual foundation but are just into socialising or church-political action. My subjective impression is that this is less the case in the English-speaking world but it's best to do some investigation for yourself in the area where you live. Also I know that queer people who have been deeply wounded by the traditional churches might find these groups 'too close to home' and want more distance from those denominations. However, others find this a place in which they are able to confront the injustice they have had to suffer.

b. Worship groups and congregations within traditional denominations

This model is about gays and lesbians forming their own worship group and using an existing church within which to invite people to celebrate worship services every week or every month, yet shying away from forming a church or denomination on their own.

This type of queer spiritual support base has been very important for me over the last 15 years. In 1991 I started a worship group like this together with my partner and a few other gay Christians in Basel, Switzerland. To my knowledge it was a pioneering project, at least in the German-speaking part of Europe. We called it the Lesbische und Schwule Basiskirche (LSBK

= Lesbian and Gay Grassroots Church) Over the years more such independent worship groups have been started and now quite a number of big cities in Switzerland and Germany have these regular worship services. They are connected in a network called Queer Gottesdienstgemeinden that freely translates into Queer Worship Communities. This kind of gay and lesbian worship group now also exists in other parts of Europe and the world. For example, in London there is a regular queer Roman Catholic worship service. Some of the groups are Roman Catholic like the one in London and another in Frankfurt; others are ecumenical. To illustrate further the possibilities of this type of queer spiritual group, I will say a bit more about the LSBK.

Lesbian and Gay Grassroots Church Basel (LSBK)
The group started because it was felt that, on the one hand, the existing local gay Christian group offered only intellectual discussion and socialising but no spiritual content and, on the other hand, local worship services were not inclusive in their liturgy and preaching. Moreover, many queer people felt too upset and insecure to mingle with the average church crowd, being put off by the exclusively heterosexual slant of the sermons etc. To reach these gays and lesbians with the Gospel, something special had to be created.

The LSBK is an ecumenical worship group. Each month (on the third Sunday of the month at 6 pm) its members celebrate a worship service together in the 'Elisabethan' City Church in Basel. In this Protestant church they are under the umbrella of the ecumenical St Elisabeth Open Church project that is supported by both the Reformed Church and the Roman Catholic Church. The City Church project was founded by a former member of the order I belong to and was inspired by St James Piccadilly Church in London.

The LSBK is open to everybody who is interested – lesbians, gays, bisexuals, parents, friends, etc. The group members create and prepare the services themselves, with a Protestant pastor or Catholic priest to celebrate Communion or the Eucharist.

During the services participants are invited to study the Bible or consider other spiritual themes; this is followed by meditation, singing and prayer. Body, mind and spirit are integrated entirely. The services address various issues, for example: What does it mean to be different? How can we integrate our sexuality with trying to live the Gospel? After the service there is a time to meet each other, talk together and enjoy a simple potluck meal.

The organisation LSBK has over forty official members, led by a board of directors. Close to a hundred men and women come more or less regularly to the worship services, so at each service there are usually at least 30–60 people in attendance, with always a few newcomers showing up. While most of the worshippers are gay or lesbian, efforts are made also to build bridges to heterosexual people, for example by inviting a priest or pastor from a local parish. On a few occasions the presence of the president (bishop) of the Reformed Church and a dean of the Roman Catholic Church has underlined the connection to the wider church. A few times a year local choirs are also invited to contribute to the service – and not just the local gay men's chorus or lesbian *a cappella* group, but also choirs from local congregations or, on one occasion, even the choir of the regional police department!

The aims of the LSBK are, in short, according to a leaflet:

- to be visible: Homosexual women and men are entitled to live their spirituality in church, without secrecy and shame. We offer worship services that are relevant for gays and lesbians.
- to accept our feelings. We offer help and advice in the process of coming out, and support each other as we try to find a homosexual identity and sense of self-esteem which can be integrated in our everyday life.
- to discover and deepen our calling: What is the special calling in our life as a gay man or lesbian woman? What is the purpose of homosexuality from the perspective of Christian spirituality?
- to celebrate our faith. We want to be a community where people

can be active in the church as well as politically. A community where we can allow our spirituality to develop and mature.

I personally think there is quite a potential to start more of these worship groups in an increasing number of cities. My experience is that it does not create a ghetto. Straight people regularly join in and certainly the existence of such a group is a challenge and a light to the wider church and to society. One main reason why the apostles were eventually convinced that 'gentiles' should be fully included in the church was because they saw the Holy Spirit at work in these people. Such open worship services are splendid opportunities to see the Holy Spirit at work in a homosexual person!

c. Independent churches and community bases

The foundation of independent denominations by gays and lesbians has been the most radical and, for many, the most controversial step yet taken. But this type of spiritual home for gays and lesbians has a huge membership worldwide, so there is an obvious need for it.

Independent churches go beyond the remit of the worship groups I described above by seeing themselves as fully established churches with a denominational status and a clergy of their own. Some do, however, model themselves after a specific denomination. On one of my journeys with my partner through the USA a few years ago, we attended a mass at a gay and lesbian Catholic church. There are also queer Pentecostal churches, Orthodox churches and even Jewish synagogues. Moreover there are individual Christian congregations that cater mainly for queer people, like the Cathedral of Hope in Dallas, Texas, which has an active membership of over two thousand. Many small gay and lesbian churches can be found in places like Hong Kong, the Philippines or Singapore.

But by far the largest and most influential institution is the worldwide fellowship of the

Metropolitan Community Churches (MCC)

MCC sees itself as ecumenical even though it tends towards the evangelical. It is certainly a pioneer within the worldwide gay and lesbian Christian movement. It was founded in Los Angeles, California, in 1968 and by 1973 the first congregation outside North America formed in London, England. The initiator of MCC, Rev. Troy Perry, started this church after he lost his job as a preacher in the Pentecostal church because he was gay. He felt called by God to start a church where homo- and bisexual people could feel safe and fully accepted. Since then some hundred more congregations have formed so that worldwide membership now stands at over 40,000 men and women. While the majority of congregations and members are in the USA, at the time of writing there are also MCCs in Canada, Mexico, Venezuela, Brazil, Argentina, Australia, New Zealand, the Philippines, South Africa, Nigeria, Germany, France, Denmark, Romania, Spain and Britain, where there are 11 churches in England and Scotland. Membership is usually made up mostly of LGB people. Many of them left their original churches because they were mistreated. Other members came originally from a secular background and found their commitment to the Christian faith through MCC.

The strong point of this model is its independence. Creating one's own church structure has many advantages. MCC is the largest predominantly queer organisation in the world. Often the member churches own property, especially in North America, which is also of use to other gay and lesbian groups. MCC is making efforts – so far unsuccessful – to become a full member of the World Council of Churches but at the moment this is being blocked by the Eastern Orthodox churches that threaten to leave the WCC if this happens. However, they have been more successful in working with local ecumenical church councils. But otherwise the energy is not used to get involved in the 'battlefield' surrounding the issue of homosexuality and the churches but rather flows fully into the ministry with and for gays and lesbians.

I remember my first visit to England and London in the

summer of 1979 where I went to my first MCC service and got a warm welcome from Rev. Hong Tan, who later served for many years as an Elder in the Universal Fellowship of MCC. Then I spent a year in the USA, mostly in Sacramento, the capital of California. This gave me the opportunity to explore all kinds of queer Christian groups and also MCC worship services and conferences. I was able to witness the enormous energy that MCC frees up in its churches and ministries. Many of its members came from conservative churches that ignore, discriminate against or hassle gay and lesbian people. MCC tends to have a strong social ministry as well.

Throughout its history MCC has often been accused of creating a religious ghetto for queer people. Of course, this is a danger and much depends on the extent to which the local church reaches out to other churches and to those heterosexual Christians who are open to dialogue and fellowship.

I was privileged to meet the founder of MCC, Rev. Troy Perry, on several occasions in California and Germany. He is still very active and influential within the worldwide fellowship of MCC churches. It's hard to ignore his American Pentecostal origins as his preaching is full of spirit, with a strong evangelical flavour. Of course, this goes along with a high sensibility for social justice issues and inclusiveness. His fervent efforts are not unlike those of Martin Luther King and similarly there have been occasions when his life too was threatened. He has written several books with autobiographical content which discuss MCC-related issues. In one of them he succinctly points out what, for him, are the three most important aspects of the Gospel, what he calls the three-pronged Gospel:

Salvation – God so loved the world that God sent Jesus to tell us that whoever believes shall not perish but have everlasting life; and 'whoever' included me as a gay male, unconditionally, because salvation is free – no church can take it away.

Community – For those who have no families who care about them, or who find themselves alone or friendless, the church will be a family.

Christian social action – We would stand up for all our rights, secular and religious, and we would start fighting the many forms of tyranny that oppressed us.

(Troy Perry, *Don't Be Afraid Anymore*, p.38)

d. Religious orders and house communities

Since 1985 I myself have been a member of a spiritual group of this kind: an ecumenical order that existed only in Switzerland at the time I entered it. The main advantage of this type of spiritual home for gays and lesbians is that it is the most committed kind of group, because you make a vow for a certain period, or for life, and/or you may literally live in community. Because of my background and, in my opinion, the great potential of this kind of group, it is no surprise that this model is very dear to me.

There were two developments in the 20th century that fostered this new form of a very old sort of religious community. First was the conviction that new kinds of orders and communities had to be created to address the urgent need for a shared vision and/or a common life. One of the communities described in this section was founded in 1938 in this kind of pioneering spirit. The other two that followed were part of a new wave of community initiatives that had its impulse in the 1960s' communal movement and the founding and flourishing of new orders such as – perhaps the most important of all – the Taizé community started by Brother Roger in Burgundy, France.

A major difference between these new communities and orders and the ancient ones like the Franciscans, Benedictines, Jesuits, etc., is that the new ones usually accept both sexes and different forms of lifestyle, not just celibates.

For me, a big advantage of belonging to an order or community is the opportunity to make a commitment to a spiritual ideal and ethos, as this is often not possible in the average congregation or group. Besides, there is likely to be a stronger fellowship with other members of the order and a more distinct encouragement and initiative towards spiritual growth. Religious orders and monasteries have played a very important and formative role in the development and spiritual life of the church throughout many centuries. But because of today's increased emphasis on individualism on the one hand, and the continuing insistence on celibacy on the other, the number of new applicants to the historical orders has gone down significantly, especially in the Western world.

It is my hope that the new orders and communities will flourish and offer a home to gay and lesbian people too.

The Iona Community

Iona is a small island off the west coast of Scotland, where in 563 Columba founded a Celtic monastery that was very influential in his own time. In the Middle Ages it was the site of a Benedictine abbey, and over the centuries the island has attracted many thousands of people on their own journey of pilgrimage. The Iona Community was founded in 1938 by the Rev. George MacLeod, then a parish minister in Glasgow who brought trainee ministers and craftsmen together each summer on Iona to rebuild the ruined abbey. It is an ecumenical Christian community that is committed to seeking new ways of living the Gospel in today's world. Although the community has a centre on Iona, most of its members live throughout Scotland and in other parts of Britain, and slowly it is spreading to a few other countries like Germany and the USA. The Iona Community remains committed to rebuilding the common life, through working for social and political change, striving for the renewal of the church with an ecumenical emphasis, and exploring new, more inclusive approaches to worship, all based on an integrated understanding of spirituality.

The Iona Community today has about 250 members, mostly in Britain, over 1500 Associate Members and around 1400 Friends worldwide; it is by far the largest community described in this section. While the community's spiritual centre is on Iona, its mainland home is in Glasgow which is the base for the community's administration, its work with young people, its magazine and Wild Goose Publications, which published the book you are reading. As an ecumenical community of men and women from different walks of life and different traditions in the Christian church, its members share a common rule which includes mutual accountability for their use of time and money, daily prayer, and reading of the Bible. Members meet regularly throughout the year in local groups and in four plenary gatherings, including a week on Iona. As a community, members corporately and individually pursue some particular areas of concern:

- Justice, peace, and the integrity of creation (opposing nuclear weapons, campaigning against the arms trade and for ecological justice).
- Political and cultural action to combat racism.
- Action for economic justice; locally, nationally and globally
- Issues in human sexuality.
- Discovering new and relevant approaches to worship.
- The deepening of ecumenical dialogue and communion and inter-religious relations.

For years now the Iona Community has also been committed to including gay men and lesbian women. While staying on Iona I met some of these members. Since the late 1990s Iona has been the host for the LGCM bi-annual retreat. In 2004 I led this week together with Iona Community member Rev. Cass Howes. It was obvious to me that the Iona Community provided a space for this group and its concerns. While the community does not have a specific gay and lesbian caucus, it was my impression that it does really welcome gay and lesbian believers. Also its wonderful worship resources give witness to a spiritual depth and a wide horizon where queer people too can contribute, feel included and be nourished. The publication of this book by the Iona Community's publishing arm further emphasises this attitude. The present leader of the community is Rev. Kathy Galloway who also shares a vision and practice of inclusiveness.

Readers who are interested in joining or becoming associated with the Iona Community may want to spend a week or so on Iona first and then find out about possible membership and a local group. Starting in 2006, I will be able to continue leading retreats on Iona following the success of the one in 2004.

Diakonische Kommunität Friedensgasse

As mentioned before, I joined this community twenty years ago. *Diakonische* means 'serving', *Kommunität* 'community', in the sense of an order, and *Friedensgasse*, 'Peace Alley' – the name of the street where the centre was located for two decades.

Inspired by the brotherhood of Taizé and the Franciscan ideal, this order was founded in 1982 by a Swiss married couple, Pierre and Catherine Brunner-Dubey, then both in their early to mid-twenties, who had a vision of the work such a community could do.

The Friedensgasse is a contemporary Christian order, a community of faith and life. It is rooted in the traditions of the Christian religion and takes an integrated spiritual approach. It is influenced by the practice of ministry diakonia or deaconry that has been in existence since the early Christian church and it embodies an ecumenical outlook. Its vision is sustained by a newly emerging Christian cosmology. It is guided by a holistic and unifying view of the world that connects the roots of the Christian faith with mysticism and spirituality in an integrated world-view. The Friedensgasse's special and contemporary challenge is to acknowledge Christ in his cosmic and universal dimension as the beginning and the end of creation, and to work together for the unity of the world as one integral organism, in which we discover the community of the body of Christ.

The inner dimension of our vocation and the heart of this spirituality is love. It is the essence and purpose of Christian faith and life. It is a kind of being which expresses itself in every aspect of our existence: as love towards God, our neighbour and our divine self, and as love towards our enemies. Love also involves a positive attitude towards the body and towards sexuality.

The outward expression of the order's vocation is a firm intention to live in solidarity with the poor and disadvantaged of this world. Focusing on this aim, Friedensgasse intends to live 'diakonia' as a message of the love of God and as a practical expression of the commandment to love. It is a specific demonstration of this inner calling and our attempt to put into action the vision of humanity and the whole of creation as the body of Christ.

Therefore the Friedensgasse carries out several different ministries. One main concern is to create a home, a place where we all find our dignity and humanity, where we can lead meaningful lives and develop and evolve in personal freedom. Lively relationships and mutually respectful friendships shape our being together in daily life, thus making the roles of strong/weak, helper/needy superfluous and dispensable.

Over the years, further ministries of spirituality, peace and dialogue with other religions have developed. To this end a retreat centre in Tuscany has been established and contacts with people and groups in countries like Britain, South Africa, Israel-Palestine and India have been formed. 'Frieden' means peace and this issue may attain more emphasis in the future.

Members of the community are connected as 'friends', 'candidates' and 'novices'. The novice eventually commits with a vow for life. In the order there are men and women living in committed partnerships and others who are single or who have chosen celibacy. As committed partnerships the order accepts marriages and also partnerships of same-sex couples. Members commit to the ethos and spirituality of the order as set out in the Rule and to social engagement and regular prayers as well as regular meetings with other members.

The year 2005 brought wide-reaching changes. After much thought, prayer and discussion the order decided to dissolve its social ministry in Basel, Switzerland. Therefore the Podere Fiorli, the Centre for Peace and Community in Tuscany, has become its new headquarters and an additional building is being planned to offer more space for community members and guests. There are now just two members in Switzerland and my partner and I are living in London for the foreseeable future, while the remaining members live in Tuscany. Pierre and Catherine still have ties to the Peace University they helped to found in Israel.

So the original set-up, with all the community members living together in the same Swiss city, has definitely dissolved and we are now a small international community with members in Italy, Switzerland and Britain. This is a challenge. Practically speaking, my partner and I are in Tuscany several times a year. At least once a year I offer retreats for gays and lesbians in this beautiful and inspiring setting. Maybe another consequence will be that a local group will form in the UK. Perhaps this book will arouse some interest. Of course, there is work to be done. For example, the rule and the liturgy of the order were laid down in books published in German a few years ago. These books would need to be translated into English. Also the members of the order must discuss whether there should be a change of name – not only because the house at the Friedensgasse has been sold, but also because this name means very little in the broader international context into which the community has now moved.

Mercy of God Community (MGC)

While both the Friedensgasse and Iona Communities were founded by straight people, the Mercy of God Community was founded by gay men and even now most members are lesbian or gay. Members and Associates can be found in many states across the USA and in various occupations and ministries, the majority on the East Coast.

The sisters and brothers live in accordance with the rule of MGC, which was founded in 1988. They profess the vows of detachment from material things, responsible sexuality and obedience to the Gospel, for which the community has developed its own practices. The members live and work locally; membership does not imply relocation. Some are single and live alone or in voluntary groupings, while others are married or in committed relationships.

All members are required to be engaged in a ministry which they choose and which the community affirms. They have to be self-supporting, through employment or in retirement, and they support the community through their stewardship. Members and associates pause for prayer, whether alone or with others, three times every day. Suggested texts are provided in the Common Prayer section of the Community Handbook. Periodically the members gather within geographic regions for prayer, spiritual growth activities, and socialising. The entire community assembles twice a year, once for a spiritual retreat in the spring and again for a chapter or conference in the fall. Wearing a religious habit is optional. For those who do so, it is an outward and tangible sign of their commitment to follow Jesus Christ and to serve his people.

I visited the MGC in Massachusetts with my partner in 1997 and we were warmly welcomed by Fr Steven Edwards and other leaders of the community. At that time there was no communal housing or centre, so it was very much up to the individual how he or she lived the rule in daily life.

A further idea that comes out of all of this – whether in relation to the particular communities we have talked about or totally independent of any of them – is the setting up of community houses. A few men and/or women rent a big house together, with private space for themselves. One of the rooms is set aside as a communal chapel/meditation room where daily liturgies or meditations can take place. This could also offer gays and lesbians the opportunity to do spiritual work together.

e. Spiritual institutes, centres and seminar groups

Over ten years ago I was excited to learn that Methodist minister Neil Whitehouse, together with Franciscan James Anthony, had started a spiritual project for gays and lesbians in London, called 'Kairos in Soho' (KiS). Neil's ultimate vision was to form a 'soul centre', a large ecumenical spiritual centre for queer people in central London. In the meantime, they were able to rent premises at the heart of the gay scene in Old Compton Road in London. In this way, they were able immediately to start offering their meditation classes, support and self-help groups, courses, counselling, etc. Neil expended a great deal of effort to raise money to finance this visionary 'soul centre'. After some reasonable hope, the National Lottery fund turned down KiS's request for a substantial grant and there were no other viable resources on the horizon. Because Neil and James's successors were partly employed by KiS there were running costs to meet. About three years ago Neil quit his job at KiS, the project that he had started, and moved to Canada. Other people are now in charge and new rooms have been rented in the Soho area. Although it has had to remain small, KiS continues to offer a highly valuable space for gays and lesbians to air spiritual issues. While at the beginning KiS had a strong Christian identity, more emphasis is now placed on non-religious spiritual offerings and inter-religious dialogue. The latter takes place in regular meetings attended and contributed to by gay and lesbian people from different religious backgrounds.

KiS offers instruction and support for personal development, holistic health, self-help and psychological issues. Its mission statement is 'to promote the mental, physical, spiritual and social well-being of lesbians, gay men and their friends'.

Inspired by Neil and KiS, in late 1997 I started a project called 'Spirituality from a gay and lesbian perspective', which I later renamed 'C-QUEER – Gays and Lesbians in Christian Spirituality'. C-QUEER was part of the educational wing of the Friedensgasse Community.

The focus of the spiritual offering of C-QUEER lies mainly in the organisation of weekend seminars, workshops and week-long retreats for gays and lesbians, but I am also available for personal counselling. Through my five-year training as a Psychosynthesis counsellor, I have acquired further skills. All the courses emphasise a deep and open Christian tradition, while central to them are themes that are relevant for gays and lesbians: questions about the purpose and the potential of life,

sexual ethics, relationship issues, dealing with wounds and healing, issues of faith, and new forms of prayer, meditation, ritual,
etc. Elements of these group meetings may include discussions,
painting, dancing, meditation, visualisation exercises and services of worship.

During the first two years the majority of the courses were
led by qualified people invited in from outside, but over the
remaining years I have conducted most courses myself, either
alone or with someone else, like renowned theologian James
Alison or London therapist Werner Valentin. At first the courses
were usually located in Basel, Switzerland and at the Podere
Fiorli in Tuscany. For the last three years I have organised
courses for English-speaking people in Tuscany and I have also
been asked to lead retreats in Britain at various centres like Iona
or Winford Manor.

Because of my move to the UK and in light of my experience
that queer people in English-speaking countries have a stronger
interest in spirituality than those in Germany, Austria and
Switzerland, I will from now on work in an English-language
context rather than a German one. And naturally I now offer
counselling where I live in England.

I was not the only one who followed Kairos in Soho's example.
A notable new major spiritual project that has sprung up in
recent years is Queer Spirit, based in San Francisco, California,
founded and led by Christian de la Huerta, writer of the excellent
book *Coming Out Spirituality*. As can be seen on his website,
Queer Spirit offers a wide range of options for gay men. Queer
Spirit does not belong to a specific religion. On the other hand
Christian strongly believes that the various religions have to be
engaged in discussion about gay and lesbian issues. He describes
this vividly in his book: he is part of the 'United Religions' effort
and in their inter-religious and intercontinental meetings he
always introduces gay and lesbian issues.

Another such organisation is the long-standing Christian
gay/lesbian spiritual project called 'Lazarus Project' in Los
Angeles, California.

f. Other types of group

One group in Britain that is difficult to classify is The Edward Carpenter Community of Gay Men. Named after English gay spiritual pioneer Edward Carpenter, ECC (founded in the 1980s) organises several weekend and week-long spiritual retreats each year. Participants are asked to contribute to these gatherings by creative means. So you may find yourself involved in chanting, meditation, drawing, acting, singing, and so on. While there are gay Christians involved in ECC, most of their events clearly define spirituality in a very broad, often non-religious sense. The gatherings are very informal. In 2004 I attended an ECC weekend in Yorkshire and found the atmosphere open, loving and casual, with a lot of space to be creative and to celebrate.

Then there are a few Christian conference centres that offer annual gay and lesbian retreats. In my own country, Switzerland, this is an old tradition. Two of the most important conference centres (one Protestant, the other Roman Catholic) have been offering such yearly events since as far back as 1973. During the 1980s I myself was involved in starting and organising a similar annual event in another big conference centre belonging to the Reformed Church. When I started to become more focused on the UK, I was amazed to find that hardly any Christian conference and retreat centres in the UK had this tradition. The exception was the Jesuit centre Loyola Hall near Liverpool, where David Birchall SJ started yearly gay and lesbian Christian retreats a couple of years ago. While on a three-month sabbatical in England during the winter of 2002–2003, I visited quite a number of interesting retreat centres and found that many are open to offering retreats for gays and lesbians but that there is a need for facilitators to take the initiative. Together with Stafford Whiteaker, author of the bestselling *The Good Retreat Guide* and other books, I did exactly that and in autumn 2004 we inaugurated the first gay and lesbian retreat at Winford Manor, Somerset, one of the best retreat centres in England. A friend of mine, Stephen Weaver, felt the same impulse and was able to facilitate the setting up of the first gay and lesbian retreat in the renowned Ammerdown Centre, while another friend, Michael Giddings, started similar retreats at the inspiring Othona Community, located on the beautiful Dorset coast. Coincidentally, in the same year the Emmaus House Centre in Bristol pioneered a retreat for lesbians and gay men. There is huge potential in Britain and beyond and I hope to take part in fostering this further now that I live in this country. It's a worthwhile effort!

As far as I know there are also centres in the USA that offer this kind of regular retreat. For instance, the ecumenical Kirkridge Centre in Pennsylvania and the Easton Mountain Retreat Centre in Upper New York come to mind, but there must be many more.

Furthermore there are some offerings from a new age or esoteric tradition. As mentioned earlier in this book, there are groups of gay males who call themselves Radical Faeries – mostly in the USA. These and similar groups are trying to revive what they consider ancient Pagan and Wicca traditions. In England there is gay spiritual retreat hotel close to Bournemouth, called Hamilton Hall. Others explore the Tantric way and offer courses in gay Tantra. But as with many straight Tantra courses, gay Tantra as offered in the Western world often has little to do with the original profound spiritual intentions of the Indian Tantric tradition and its spiritual depth leaves something to be desired.

After reflecting on all these types of spiritual community for gays and lesbians I want to make it clear that these home bases do not exist so that we can retreat from the world or create ghettos. If we follow the Christian understanding of all of humanity as the Body of Christ, it is important for individuals and committed groups to network with others and be open to each other. The existence of specific spiritual safe places for queer people does not diminish the importance of larger and broader church organisations. But the above-mentioned types of spiritual community for queer people do all offer vital ingredients. They allow us

- to explore the potential resulting from our sexual orientation
- to exist in a space where our gifts and callings as gays and lesbians can be explicitly fostered and supported
- to have room to experience healing when we have been wounded through homophobia
- to experience solidarity with other gays and lesbians on our spiritual path
- to discover rituals, worship services, and forms of prayer and meditation that are relevant for queer people
- to reflect on how we deal with our sexuality so that we can learn to live it in a mature, dignified and loving way and to support same-sex couples in their relationships
- to explore what a mature Christian spirituality can offer to queer people

In many countries there is still the need and potential for new groups and I hope that this book will encourage some readers to start one.

One question that I have been asked repeatedly is: Shall I leave my traditional church or order where I have experienced so much homophobia? I think the answer to this question is a very individual one. I personally do not advocate that every gay man or lesbian woman should leave the Roman Catholic Church, the Anglican Communion, etc., because of the homophobic attitudes that still prevail at every level. There are actually many queer people out there who have done just that – they have quit religion for good – and because of this a number of them speak very negatively when it comes to the subject of spirituality. Whether you remain in the church or not, you should ask yourself several questions, and you have to ask them in relation to your existing congregation or group and not in the first instance with the Vatican in mind:

- How far is this congregation, this order, this community, a place where I experience solidarity, where the threefold command of love is taught and lived?

- Are my talents appreciated and can I freely and creatively use them in this setting?
- Is this a place where I am accepted, where I can evolve and where my energies can flow fully?

As I reasoned before, it is essential to have a visible group of people amongst whom I can feel at home and grow. How traditional or experimental the setting is – that's less important. I think such living cells are essential for the church of the future and the survival of the world in general. I love the image of the rainbow. Every colour has its place. But to find its place it must first radiate its own pure nature. In queer spiritual groups this process is visible. The gay and lesbian colours can glow and radiate, can be painted with bold brush-strokes. In that way too our heterosexual brothers and sisters in spirit can see our colours clearly and accept them thankfully. I am grateful for the rich and varied colours of the Kingdom of God. Every colour can shine!

QUESTIONS

Which of the types of groups and communities presented in this chapter have attracted you most?

Have you learnt anything important on your spiritual life journey through relationships with others?

What part do worship services play in your life? When you look for a spiritual home, how important are religious services and rituals for you?

What expectations do you have in relation to rituals, liturgies and services? Are you willing to contribute to such celebrations and acts of worship?

Which existing group could you imagine yourself joining? Or would you prefer to start a new one? How about it?

SUGGESTIONS

Search for and meditate on a Bible passage that talks about community and the image of the body of Christ, e.g. 'You are the body of Christ; when one member suffers, all suffer ...'

Take some time to search the internet for information about queer spiritual groups. Enter phrases such as 'gay spirituality', 'lesbian Christians' or 'queer Buddhists' into the search engines. You will be amazed at the variety of information that comes up. There are also link suggestions at the end of this book.

EXERCISE

Movement meditation:
Community council of the gay and lesbian tribe

This exercise is based on an unusual and challenging concept: the image of gays and lesbians as a 'tribe'. A few lesbian and more so gay authors use the word 'tribe' to signify and describe the gay and lesbian community. John R. Stowe uses this concept in his powerful book *Gay Spirit Warrior*, as does also Andrew Ramer in his unusual book *Two Flutes Playing*.

Before you begin this exercise you should choose some meditative, calming music: choral music, new age music, soft world music, or flute, harp, piano or other suitable classical music. If it has lyrics, they should not distract you. Don't play it too loud. If you prefer absolute silence, you may of course do this exercise that way too. If you wish, begin with a short prayer that invokes a blessing on your space so that the exercise will be healing and positive. Also make sure that no one will disturb you.

a) First of all, stand still in the middle of the room and close your eyes. Be aware that the space around you is holy. This is a sacred and protected room. Honour your connection with all life by visualising roots from the centre of your being going deep into the earth. Now imagine that a clear, bright light surrounds you. This light comes down from above. It is a divine light that fills both you and the room. Thank Christ for his support, protection and warmth.

b) Tune in to your body. Focus on the in and out of your breath. How do you feel inside? Connected? Scattered? Are you all in your head or can you direct and extend your awareness to other parts of your body? Take time to become conscious of every part of yourself. Breathe with awareness for a little while until you feel ready to begin the movement.

Now begin to move your body gently, in whatever way feels right. Which parts of you feel loose and relaxed? Where do you feel tight?

Take a little time to shake out tight muscles and to stretch and move as you please until you feel aligned and ready to go deeper.

c) First, ask your body to remind you how it feels to be alone and unconnected. 'Show me how it feels to be isolated and lonely.' Watch how your body responds and what feelings come up. Does it feel intimate and comfortable? Familiar? Natural? Exaggerate the movement your body is making for a few moments – bring it into your face, hands, back, pelvis, feet – all over. See where it takes you.

d) Relax again and feel calmness return to your body. Breathe regularly. Move gently and visualise a sacred space, outdoors, in a magnificent landscape – perhaps on top of a hill, on a sandy beach, in a field, in a circle of trees. Take your time to let the details come – the view from the top of the mountain, the warmth of the earth beneath your feet, the breeze on your skin. Enjoy this holy space, for here is where you meet the rest of your tribe.

e) Now make a clear request – 'Show me my connection with the Tribe of Men who Love Men' (or 'Women who Love Women', or 'Tribe of Men who Love Men and Women who Love Women'). See yourself moving into a great circle of gay men (or lesbian women, or queer men and women). Feel how alive the energy is here, how strong, supportive, nurturing and loving.

Continue to move and make your movements a little bigger. What images come to your inner eye? Look around you at the faces within the Tribe. You may recognise some of them. Others will be new. Some will be old, some will be young, or in-between, and some may have different skin colours than others.

Notice what the members of the tribe are wearing. Some may be wearing very little; others have beautiful costumes and jewellery. Imagine what you are wearing to reflect the glory of your own wholeness.

f) Visualise yourself holding hands with the others in a large circle. Feel how much loving strength flows from one hand to the next around the circle. Feel it touch you, fill you, and nurture the places in you that have felt abandoned and alone.

This is your Tribe, where you belong. You have been in this place before and can return any time you wish. The energy of this tribal connection nurtures you all the time. Knowing this, ask your body, 'Show me how it feels to know that I am always supported by the Tribe.' Give your whole self to the movement. Move for as long as you like.

g) You are still moving in the circle of your Tribe. You are safe and secure, held and yet free. You now become aware that a divine light is shining down on the whole Tribe, including you.

Remember that you also need a community in your daily life – a real physical experience of loving, caring, wise people. You know that there are several possible types of spiritual group where you will be fully accepted and recognised as a gay man or a lesbian woman. You now have the chance to ask the other Tribe members which kind of spiritual group you need in your present life situation. Listen to the answer that comes from the Tribe.

Maybe they mention a specific group which you already know well. Or perhaps they suggest one of the possible types of group, like an order or community, a queer worship group, a gay/lesbian church, a traditional but accepting congregation, a spiritual centre, a gay/lesbian Christian support group, etc.

You may get an answer in words and/or symbols. Whatever the answer you receive, show your gratitude. You'll have enough time later to explore the answer.

h) If you feel the need to ask another question about your life situation or your being queer, you may take the time to do so now.

i) Thank the Tribe for showing you the connections. Now let go of the images of the Tribe and the sacred place, knowing that you can return to them at any time. Focus on your body and your breath and let your body move. Maybe you want to dance for a few minutes but then let your movement come gently to rest. Let all the energy you have generated flow down through your feet, out through your roots, and into the Earth, where it brings strength and health.

j) When you feel grounded and clear, open your eyes and go over your experience, reflecting on it. You may do this standing, sitting or lying down, but stay fully awake and aware. How was your connection? What did you learn? How did the members of the Tribe look and feel to you? How did it feel to hold hands, to be part of the tribal circle? What answers did you get to your question or questions? Which type of spiritual organisation or practical local group did they suggest? What does that all mean for your life and future?

(The exercise is based on one by John R. Stowe in his book *Gay Spirit Warrior*, pp.91–93)

PRAYER

Cosmic Christ,

I thank you
that I belong to the gay and lesbian Tribe.
I thank you
that this Tribe is part of the Human Family as you intended it.
I thank you
for the broad and colourful body of humanity.

I ask you
to guide me on my journey
towards other human beings, groups,
communities, and centres,
where I can unfold freely and employ my talents.
Move me,
if you give me the call,
to start a new group by myself or with others.
I want to move and evolve in my life.
Give me wisdom and strength.

Amen

Eleven

Where Do We Go from Here?

Not all of us are called to be saints, bodhisattvas, and world transformers. But we participate in the collective transformation of consciousness whether we mean to or not. It is not so much the behaviour of individual gay people as it is the appearance of gay identification itself that conveys the message. Any of us can become aware of what we are doing in planetary evolution. And we can choose to live our lives according to these metaphors. In so doing, we change the world. We ease the suffering in the world by putting out good gay vibes. We ease our own suffering by recognising eternity in every moment. [...]

Gay people are in the vanguard of a transformation in consciousness. We participate in waking up the planet by calling to important spiritual, psychological, and ecological issues. We help reveal the workings of Gaia. We test religion and we help redefine God. We stand on the ledge of the world's weird wall. We are oracles. We are guides. We put out good intentions. We radiate good vibes. We are moved by spirits true. And we are spirits true.

(Toby Johnson, *Gay Spirituality* p.270)

All change happens only in the present moment. That is the only part of my life that is fully in my grasp and available for my choice of action. The only time I can really fully live is now. It is obvious that not all promises about the future will be kept by any means, and it is a waste of time to dwell constantly on visions of things to come. As enlightening as those visions may be, they should not distract us from living in the here and now and making decisions and acting upon them.

We all use phrases like 'I will try ...' or 'I intend to ...' but they can be traps. If a decision is pushed into the future over and over again, it loses its power and conviction and in the end nothing worthwhile is achieved. We are in danger of procrastinating. Now is the moment of power and decision! I myself have experienced how good intentions can degenerate into harmless fantasies when I shirk responsibility for my life and block real decisions and processes. We narrow our horizons not only by constantly dwelling on the past but also by continuously thinking about the future – whether happily or anxiously.

As has become clear in this book, by 'living in the present' I do not mean living a hedonistic and indulgent life. If you know the unforgettable and poignant classic Fellini movie *La Dolce Vita* you will be aware of the big difference. It's not about a 'sweet life' that results from giving in to every decadence and compulsion, driven by all the urges and subpersonalities of the hour. Living in the here and now means life lived in the fullness of the present moment, in deep connection with one's divine origin. The philosophy of existentialism points in a similar direction.

When I wrote in the previous chapters about the future of the gay and lesbian movement and about following a path of personal development, I wanted to make these points based on the understanding that when we look into the future, collectively or alone, when we open ourselves up to dreams and visions, we always need to stay connected with the present. Because it is only in our present life that we stand at the crossroads and choose our path into the future. Over and over again.

Let us now outline some of the aspects and points we have considered and see what this might imply for the collective situation of gays and lesbians, and especially the queer spiritual movement in the English-speaking world.

When I wrote the original German version of this book I had to include information about what was happening in English-speaking countries. In Germany the publication of a queer spiritual book is a fairly rare event and just a handful of good theological books on the issue are in print. Gay Christian groups in Germany, Switzerland and Austria are still top-heavy on theological discussion and seem to meet together solely on a casual basis; only the last decade has seen the birth of a few gay/lesbian spiritual groups in those countries.

People who live in North America, the British Isles, Australasia and South Africa, or in other parts of the world but are fluent in English, now have extensive access to a wide range of first-rate spiritual and theological gay/lesbian literature. Some of these books are classics which have been in print for decades; others are just now being published. One too often hears of anti-gay fundamentalists in the USA and other places and forgets about the great network, the many groups and organisations of gay and lesbian Christians and queer people of different spiritual persuasions. So already there are things to celebrate.

Let's widen our focus to the general gay and lesbian movement: As much as it has achieved so far (in the way of rights, for example), at least in most of the Western world, it is still to some degree immature – it is in a crisis of perspective and certainly has some way to go. The consciousness of this important movement needs to be expanded. So, what would be an evolutionary step for this movement, a development that needs to take place in the years or decades to come?

- The awareness that being queer is much more than just a matter of sex. The other two levels need to be taken into account: what being gay or lesbian means in the sense of love partnerships and especially what it means to have a different, queer consciousness that can be used to serve humanity and the world, to help change them for the better.

- The incredible reservoir of energy and capability visible in all its colours at gay and lesbian parades and parties needs to be expanded and refocused more keenly into other dimensions: artistic, social, political, spiritual, sociological and so on.

- The spiritual journey for queer people does not bypass the dark side of life. We have to acknowledge that the gay scene too has its destructive patterns – the abusive and degrading use of sexuality, consumerism, addiction, the cult of youth, and so on.

- As in other periods and cultures, queer people with their rich capabilities in the areas of spirituality, the arts and education have a special role in pioneering new directions in the development of consciousness. In this let us be inspired by historical same-sex traditions (such as that of the North American native population) even if we cannot directly reproduce them. This special calling of gays and lesbians has to be poured into the cultural vessels of the present moment.

- The Christian churches – and we can extend the following assumption to all traditional world religions – need a complete reorientation and transformation. As far as the question of gay and lesbian pastors, priests, bishops, etc., is concerned, the point in the end is not so much whether queer persons can take on these roles; it is rather that gays and lesbians are specifically predestined to fulfil them. When an increasing number of openly gay and lesbian clergy and others leave their mark on the church (with more and more women in general undertaking substantial functions at all levels), then this will change the institution. Fundamentalists know this instinctively and that is one of the main reasons why they fight so bitterly and hysterically against the full participation of openly queer people and women in general. When the church becomes more inclusive, it will be less hierarchical and patriarchal. It will be more centred, artistic and warm; less deadening, top-heavy and simple-minded. Of course, it is still an open question as to how the traditional church structure will revitalise itself in the 21st century – or whether indeed the Community of Jesus will reinvent itself into new and very different structures at all. In any case, it goes without saying that even if the present organisational structures were to fall apart without being replaced, the Holy Spirit would move in unexpected ways to create appropriate new forms.

- Gay and lesbian people do not exist just for their own sake but also to serve the world. Homosexuality is not an accident but a gift. Humanity (and with it the planet itself) is presently experiencing the most challenging crisis of its history. There is a lot at stake. We will either destroy ourselves in the next few decades or we will take a new step in human consciousness (from a mental to an integral consciousness, as Ken Wilber and others call it). It will be a heightening of awareness and an expansion of mind that will have ethical consequences.

Queer people have a role to play in this. Time is pressing. Our power, imagination, wisdom and thirst for action are vital.

How can Queer Power serve the world? Here are some ways to engage in action:

- Solidarity with lesbians and gays outside of the Western world is needed more than ever. Thank God for Amnesty International which for years has had a subgroup for the dignity and human rights of sexual minorities. We need all our imagination, energy and power to help to change the fact that in roughly half the world's countries LGB persons are still imprisoned, tortured, beaten or murdered (including by the state in the form of capital punishment) because of their different sexual orientation and non-violent sexuality. It is shameful that things like that still happen in the 21st century and they have to be challenged. There is also an urgent need to stimulate debate about sexuality in those African, Asian and South American countries where the subject is still too much of a taboo. A positive and challenging examination of it would not only reduce homophobia but would also have a constructive effect on AIDS education, family planning and women's liberation.

- The aforementioned crisis endangers humanity and with it our planet. This turbulence has a tangible and dramatic face: population explosion, extreme poverty and hunger, water shortages, terrorist acts, danger from weapons of mass destruction through wars, accidents or attacks, global warming with all its possible disastrous consequences, and all the further apocalyptic damage to the environment like the cutting down of the rainforests. All human beings are asked to be aware of this and to act accordingly by joining groups, voting, protesting, educating, envisioning, etc. Within this context queer people too are asked to listen to their calling and contribute to the healing of this situation.

- From Sri Aurobindo of India to Teilhard de Chardin of Europe and Ken Wilber of America, many consciousness researchers and explorers have realised that an important step in consciousness development would be – to put it simply – to acknowledge unity in diversity. I think gays and lesbians can contribute to this process to a significant degree.

As I have demonstrated several times in this book, the queer movement must develop on three levels:

1. At grassroots level and individually: through coming out and coming in as a personal process of liberation.
2. On the collective level as a gay and lesbian community or 'tribe' (in relation to the rest of the human family) – an important movement throughout this historical period.
3. On a universal level: discovering our calling and living our potential within this world.

Let us return to our personal and daily sphere. My wish is that this book will not only kindle in you feelings of joy, awe, enthusiasm, anger or hope, but that it will also help you to expand your consciousness and encourage you to take definite steps in your life. If you have read this book up to here, you have – just by reading it and more so by trying out the meditations, exercises and prayers at the end of each chapter – already started on this process. So what further concrete steps can you take? How can you, as a gay man, a lesbian woman, deepen your spiritual journey and foster your development? Here are some ideas and suggestions.

- Repeat the exercises in this book several times or even regularly over a period of several months. Keep a written record of what happens during and after these sessions. Or you may wish to read some parts of the book meditatively before prayer, or highlight key statements or conclusions. Work with this book in a local gay and lesbian spiritual group.

- Create a shrine or meditation/prayer corner in your flat or house, as a spiritual base in your home.

- Decide on a form of meditation or prayer that you can and will do at certain times. If you cannot find a time that suits you every day, mark the different times in your diary each week as you would do with other appointments. In this way you will strengthen your relationship with God in you and with the Cosmic Christ.

- Attend a spiritual retreat at least once a year. If you have decided on a specific meditation practice (like Zen, centring prayer, etc), look for support in local meditation groups.

- It may make sense to look for your own spiritual director. This person should either be homosexual or bisexual herself or himself or, if heterosexual, have a clear, educated, open and absolutely accepting attitude towards same-sex love. In spite of the homophobic statements that are still thrown around by certain religious figures, there are now plenty of spiritual directors within the Christian tradition who are open towards gays and lesbians. Alternatively, you may prefer a counsellor or therapist, in which case you must make sure that this person has a spiritual perspective. I myself offer Psychosynthesis counselling and I know that there are many men and women from this and other transpersonal psychology traditions that have both a spiritual perspective and an awareness of gay and lesbian issues. If you feel that there are great blocks and agonies in your life that may have do to with overwhelmingly destructive situations in your past, it might be advisable to go into some form of psychotherapy. If you have problems with accepting and caring for your body, a dance therapy or body-oriented therapy could help. What you choose will depend on your situation. But certainly, if we seriously consider ourselves to be on a spiritual journey, there will be times (and sometimes for the whole of our life) when we need some support and direction.

- Seek out a spiritual community, group or congregation where you feel at home and at ease, where you are challenged and can evolve. This can be a core community, an order or a local

church. If you have just left a homophobic and abusive religious organisation, or for other reasons, you may prefer a
church group that is predominately or exclusively gay and
lesbian. Whatever your choice, make sure you choose an affirming spiritual core group. The larger organisation it belongs to
may still be homophobic (like the Roman Catholic Church) but
the community you choose must itself be affirming. Anything
else is pure masochism. In Chapter 10 I gave plenty of suggestions from which to choose, and at the end of the book there
are numerous addresses to help you make a start.

- If you choose a group or community where you are just about
the only openly gay and lesbian person, I think it's important to
connect in different ways with queer people interested in spirituality, such as through a local queer spiritual group or gay and
lesbian retreats. It is to be hoped that these will also allow you
to reflect about your potential and gifts as a queer person.

- An essential part of my own journey of faith has been the
chance to be actively involved on many occasions in a team
that organises and facilitates worship services. I have found it
a tremendous opportunity not just to participate passively in
a service but also to take an active part in the service or even
to invent new forms of worship, as I did when I was instru-
mental for ten years in creating what we called 'experimental
worship services'. Whatever the possibilities in your own situation – be it in a Bible study group, an alternative worship
service or anywhere else – use your creativity; make use of
your spiritual gifts.

- Read good spiritual literature regularly. There are many great
books that have been written by people like Richard Rohr,
Henry Nouwen and so on. You will find a bibliography at the
end of this book.

- Consider what it means to live your potential in your professional life and in your relationships and find out if you need
to make any changes to allow this to happen. In some cases
this may even lead to a change of career.

- Become aware of your talents and callings. Make a decision for a practical engagement in life on behalf of your gay brothers and lesbian sisters and also for all the human family and creation.

With these suggestions and ideas I want to invite you to return over and over again to the sacred place of silence within you, the divine source where Christ is waiting for you. Through worship, silent prayer and meditation you have the tools for this path. Be calm and silent and listen! With this attitude you will progress on your journey.

All spiritual traditions come down to the same purpose: to let go of the 'ego' so that the 'Higher Self' can dwell in us. That is the new birth, the being 'born again'. In Christian terms it is living out of the spirit, out of Christ in you as the Holy Scripture calls it.

Letting go of the ego means letting go of an old identity, of a view and attitude towards life that hinders us from living to the full; it means letting go of whatever we are addicted to in our confused, dependent, shackled state of being, where we try to fill our emptiness with all kinds of sensations and consumer products. It means letting go of a one-dimensional approach to life where, for example, we value people according to their sexual attractiveness or we think that the only important thing in life is 'success'. Letting go of all these things is very liberating.

The 'I' is very important as the 'conductor' of our life, helping us to sense and use our willpower. But the symphony we are asked to play has been composed by the Universal Christ. The notes are the material we are made of. Gay and lesbian notes have their place in this symphony. They are part of our originality and creation, and a gift for the entire world.

The Way of Christ (see Chapter 9) supports us in understanding our life, and in dealing with suffering, so that we find our true identity and calling, and shape and celebrate our life in hope. On this journey we discover our potential as gays and lesbians and the talents that go along with that. For this we learn to be thankful, and out of this gift and this thankfulness we organise our lives and enrich the world.

Where does this path lead? That is impossible to predict. We have to travel on in trust. Life is an adventure: wild and calm, loud and silent, full of both sorrow and joy. But beyond all those dualities, and in the space between all sound, lies the divine reality.

QUESTIONS

Having read the conclusions of this chapter, what will you do now in your life?

When will you do it?

How will you do it?

Will you succeed in reaching these goals?

What obstacles might you encounter?

How will you overcome those obstacles to reach your goals?

Within what time-frame do you want to realise your aims?

If you don't reach your objectives within the time-frame, what options do you have?

(These questions are from the course documents of the Institute of Psychosynthesis, Sascha Dönges, Basel. Borrowed from Sir John Whitmore: *Coaching for Performance: A Practical Guide to Growing Your Own Skills*)

SUGGESTIONS

In your imagination, visualise a positive future for yourself. Where do you want to be in five years' time from now?

Also visualise a positive future for our planet. How would humankind live if it succeeded in taking a major evolutionary step in consciousness during the 21st century? What role would LGB people play in this context of a renewed human family?

Make a list of what you have learned from this book. Become aware of any dreams, new steps and practical consequences that are developing in your life.

EXERCISE

Wisdom cards

Buy a set of wisdom cards. They are stocked by large mainstream bookshops or good spiritual ones. Most of them come under the heading of Tarot cards, like the Osho-Zen Tarot set. Take your time and select a card set you feel comfortable with and from which you sense a good energy. Use your intuition! I know there is a huge range to choose from. In German there is now also a Christian Tarot set available which uses characters from the Bible, and there is even one on the web that uses gay images. If, because of your religious background or for other reasons, you have a big problem with the Tarot tradition, consider other forms of wisdom card such as the increasingly popular Angel cards.

Back at home, set aside some time when you will not be disturbed and spread all the cards out on the floor face down. It may be helpful then to light a candle and centre yourself with a prayer (e.g. one from this book, the Lord's prayer, the peace prayer of St Francis, or Psalms 23, 73 or 139).

Become aware of the questions this book has raised and which ones have touched and moved you personally. Now ask yourself what the next step in your life could be. What theme is now ready to blossom, to take its place in your life journey?

Have a look at the cards spread out in front of you. Maybe there is a card that mysteriously attracts you. I once had an experience where I somehow saw a kind of 'glow' coming from one particular card. Or just trust your intuition and pick up the first one you notice. Take some time to look at the image and the word on this card. Think about what it might have to do with your life and in what direction the answer could lie.

Here are three further suggestions for questions you may want to ask before taking cards:

- What issues are facing me in the way I deal with my sexuality?
- What special gift in connection with my being lesbian or gay do I want to allow to evolve in my life?
- What spiritual issue is important in the next 12 months of my life?

Please be careful and respectful when doing this exercise and when using wisdom cards in general. You can learn a lot about yourself from them – about your goals, your development and relevant life issues. But they are not an oracle to be consulted on every decision you have to make. Don't become totally dependent on wisdom cards. As St Paul said: 'Test everything, keep what is good.'

PRAYER

Christ says:
'In the rainbow you see how close and faithful I am to you,
My gay brothers and lesbian sisters.
This sign of reconciliation and hope shall shine anew in the world.
Live the sign of the rainbow.
You have all the colours within you –
as reflected in the chakras.
Let the power of My Spirit rise in you,
pervading all colours.
Be a rainbow for this world!'

Christ, my brother,
both within me and encompassing the cosmos,
I thank You for the sign of the rainbow.
I dance with joy, I am carried away.
I ask You to support me and inspire me to live,
to live the colours and the message of the rainbow;
to discover the rainbow in all things big and small
and to spread the message.

Holy powerful Spirit, driver of evolution:
Through fire of sun and water of rain
You paint the rainbow in the sky.

You are fire and water in me.
Fire of my power that surrounds my sexuality,
ascend my spine
engulf my chakras and my senses.
Holy Spirit, burn in me,
drive me to utter passion for this life.

Holy powerful Spirit, you are the water
that makes me lucid, clears my mind,
that renews my thinking, immerses me in wisdom.
With fire and water, with passion and wisdom,
hasten the evolution of humankind.

In the mundane decisions and situations that await me
let me be aware of being Your daughter or son,
Father and Mother in heaven.
I devote myself to You and give myself to life.
Be tender with me, shape me, mould me,
so that I become ever more human,
the person I am meant to be.
May the calling and purpose of my life on earth
take shape in You.

Amen

Recommended Reading

Instead of just presenting a dry list of the books that I have used and recommend, I want to mention some of them in particular and give a short description. The rest I will list in alphabetical order.

A) Annotated bibliography

Classic gay and lesbian spiritual literature – Holy scriptures for queer believers

Of all the great spiritual books on queer issues that have appeared especially in the last 35 years, the majority of them have been written from a Christian perspective. What follows is a selected and annotated list of books which I consider essential or unique. To the best of my knowledge all the titles in this section are in print and can be ordered through good bookstores or the big internet booksellers like Amazon. There are also specifically gay/lesbian booksellers like A Different Light (www.adlbooks.com) or Gay's The Word (http://freespace.virgin.net/gays.theword/index.htm).

Some LGB Christian organisations like the Lesbian and Gay Christian Movement sell good books on these issues (www.lgcm.org).

Books from a Christian perspective

John McNeill: *Taking a Chance on God: Liberating Theology for Gays, Lesbians and their Lovers, Families and Friends*, Boston 1998, Beacon Press.

McNeill is probably the most important personality of the 20th century within the queer-Christian spectrum. All his other books are classics too and are highly recommended, especially *Freedom, Glorious Freedom*. He offers an intelligent, stimulating and prophetic view on all the questions and issues that might concern gay and lesbian Christians. He writes from the heart and does not shy away from including his own joyful and painful life experiences.

Chris Glaser: *Come Home. Reclaiming Spirituality and Community as Gay Men and Lesbians*, New York 1990, HarperCollins.

Glaser is presently the most distinctive gay Christian author in the USA. He has a splendid understanding of how a profound Christian spirituality, theology and biblical meditations can be brought together with the reality of LGB people. All his books are absolutely invaluable.

John Fortunato: *Embracing the Exile*, New York 1982, Seabury Press.

This classic was written over two decades ago and yet it remains a timeless work. Gay Christian and psychotherapist Fortunato has succeeded in showing the healing power of Christian spirituality in the lives of queer people. He describes the opportunities that can spring from our being wounded and exiled.

Kittredge Cherry & Zalmon Sherwood: *Equal Rites: Lesbian and Gay Worship Ceremonies and Celebrations*, Louisville 1995, Westminster John Knox Press.

A fantastic collection of rituals, worship service liturgies and other forms of religious celebration for gays and lesbians.

Glen O'Brien: *Praying from the Margins: Gospel Reflections of a Gay Man*, Dublin 2001, The Columba Press.

A small book, yet large on wisdom. O'Brien illustrates passages from the Gospel for gay men.

Elisabeth Stuart: *Daring to Speak Love's Name: A Gay and Lesbian Prayer Book*, London 1992, Hamish Hamilton.

A handy book with moving prayer suggestions for the gay/lesbian context.

Gay/lesbian books from different spiritual perspectives

Andrew Ramer: *Two Flutes Playing – A Spiritual Journeybook for Gay Men*, San Francisco 1997/2005, Lethe Press.

The only 'channelled' gay book known to me. Even if you do not believe that holy gay beings from the spiritual world gave Ramer the content, it is still possible to profit from reading this unusual book. There are a few questionable parts, but it also offers passages of great wisdom on the origin, intention, purpose and goal of gay/lesbian existence.

Thomas Thompson: *Gay Soul – Finding the Heart of Gay Spirit and Nature* (with 16 writers, healers, teachers, and visionaries), New York 1995, HarperCollins.

An extraordinary collection of contemporary gay mystics and other competent men reflecting powerfully on their spiritual experience and the context of their homosexuality and its potential. I wish a woman would put together a similar book from a lesbian point of view. Having said that, this book could also be very interesting for lesbians.

Christian de la Huerta: *Coming Out Spirituality – The Next Step* (foreword by Matthew Fox), New York 1999, Tarcher/Putnam.

De la Huerta is the founder of Queer Spirit, a project in San Francisco. In his book he puts forward an impressively expansive view of queer spirituality. A unique aspect is the description of his activity in inter-religious dialogue as an openly gay man. Apart from a problematic chapter on sexuality, this is a challenging book with many practical implications.

Peter Sweasey: *From Queer to Eternity: Spirituality in the Lives of Lesbian, Gay & Bisexual People*, London 1997, Cassell.

This British book is a pioneer in the European context. It gives a voice to lesbians and gays from numerous different religious convictions, like Christians of various denominations, Jews, Hindus, Buddhists, Sikhs, New Agers, etc. It provides an exemplary overview of the religious diversity that exists within the homosexual world.

Toby Johnson: *Gay Perspective: Things Our Homosexuality Tells Us About The Nature of God and the Universe*, Los Angeles 2003, Alyson Publications.

As in his first great spiritual book *Gay Spirituality*, Johnson offers important and far-reaching insights into the gifts of being queer from a spiritual perspective. Johnson was for many years the editor of the stimulating and unique gay spiritual journal *The White Crane* (www.whitecranejournal.com).

John R. Stowe: *Gay Spirit Warrior. An Empowering Workbook for Men Who Love Men*, Findhorn Press, Findhorn 1999.

An inspiring book that uses the gay male archetypes as its basis and includes many useful exercises.

J. Michael Clark: *Doing The Work Of Love. Men & Commitment In Same-Sex Couples*, Harriman 1999, Men's Studies Press.

Sometimes a bit complex but nevertheless a first-rate book on same-sex partnerships, their challenges, gifts and opportunities. Also includes a ritual of blessing.

Catherine Lake: *ReCreations. Religion and Spirituality in the Lives of Queer People*, Toronto 1999, Queer Press Non-Profit Community Publishing.

This is a smart collection of the different religious paths of a wide variety of lesbians and gay men – Muslim, Christian, Jewish and Buddhist.

Other recommended books

General spiritual books. Of course, books written without a specifically queer perspective can also enrich the spiritual life of gays and lesbians. Here is a subjective list of authors – most of them straight – who offer a remarkable and deep spirituality with wide horizons: Matthew Fox, Bede Griffiths, Andrew Harvey, Anthony de Mello, Thomas Merton, Henry Nouwen, Richard Rohr, Daniel J. O'Leary, David Steindl-Rast, Ralph S. Marston, Jr., Kathy Galloway, Thomas Moore, M. Scott Peck, Jim Cotter, Virginia Ramey Mollenkott.

In addition, the publisher of this book, Wild Goose Publications (www.ionabooks.com) offers a wide range of good Christian books.

Let me just point to a few very special books that have influenced and nourished me over the past few years:

Andrew Harvey: *Son of Man: The Mystical Path to Christ*, New York 1998, Tarcher.

This is an important book about Christian spirituality written by an openly gay mystic. As with most of his books, this one is highly original, and it includes practical tools to enhance one's relationship with Christ.

John Martin Sahajananda: *You Are The Light: Rediscovering the Eastern Jesus*, Alresford 2003, O Books.

Martin is a friend of mine and led the ashram in South India that was made famous by the great 20th-century mystic Bede Griffiths. Martin offers a highly original and moving view of the Gospel, especially on the point that Jesus didn't just say that He is the light of the world, he also said that we are the light of the world.

Stafford Whiteaker: *Living the Sacred: Ten Gateways to Open Your Heart*, London 2000, Rider (Random House).

I was privileged to lead a retreat for gay men together with Stafford and I hope that more will follow. This is a wonderful book for getting in touch with your spiritual self and it offers a wealth of valuable practical suggestions.

Daniel J. O'Leary: *Passion for the Possible: A Spirituality of Hope for a New Millennium*. Dublin 2002, Columba Press.

This is the kind of Christian spirituality we need in this troubled first century of the new millennium. A very profound and gifted book with challenging personal reflections.

I have frequently mentioned **Psychosynthesis** in my book. For further exploration I highly recommend the books by Piero Ferrucci and Psychosynthesis founder Roberto Assagioli. In addition, books by Diana Whitmore, Molly Young Brown and Will Parfitt deserve attention. See also Davies: *Pink Therapy 2* in book list below.

For the **evolutionary world-view** the ambitious books by Andrew Cohen, Ken Wilber, Pierre Teilhard de Chardin and Jean Gebser are recommended; also Peter Spink's *Beyond Belief – 21st Century Spirituality*, Bristol 2001, Omega Trust Publications; and one written by a contemporary gay man: Jim Marion: *Putting on the Mind of Christ: The Inner Work of Christian Spirituality*, USA 2002, Hampton Roads.

B) Other recommended titles

James Alison:
- *On Being Liked*, London 2004, Herder & Herder.
- *Faith Beyond Resentment – Fragments Catholic and Gay*, London 2001, Crossroad General Interest.

Donald L. Bolsvert: *Sanctity and Male Desire: A Gay Reading of Saints*, Cleveland 2004, Pilgrim Press.

John Boswell: *Same-Sex Unions in Premodern Europe*, New York 1994, Villard Books.

Catherine Brunner-Dubey: *Die Quelle in Dir darf singen -Neue Gebete und Liturgien für das ganz Jahr*, München 1998, Kösel Verlag.

Pierre & Catherine Brunner-Dubey: *Kraftvoll Einkehren: Eckpfeiler für eine neue Kirche*, Luzern 1996, Rex Verlag.

Edward Carpenter: *Selected Writings*, London 1984, GMP Publishers.

Richard Cleaver: *Know My Name: A Gay Liberation Theology*, Louisville 1995, Westminster John Knox Press.

Rosemary Curb & Nancy Manahan: *Lesbian Nuns – Breaking Silence*, London 1993, Nalad Press.

Liz Dale: *Coming Over & Coming Home: The Gay Near-Death Experience as Spiritual Transformation*, Houston 2001, Emerald Ink Publishing.

Dominic Davies & Charles Neal: *Pink Therapy 2*, Buckingham UK & Philadelphia 2000, Open University Press. Therapeutic perspective on working with lesbian, gay and bisexual clients (with chapter by

Keith Sylvester from a Psychosnythesis perspective).

James L. Empereur SJ: *Spiritual Direction and the Gay Person*, New York 1998, Continuum.

John Gettings: *Couples: A Photographic Documentary of Gay & Lesbian Relationships*, Hanover NH 1996, University Press of New England.

Chris Glaser:
- *Reformation of the Heart – Seasonal Meditations for Gay Christians*, Louisville 2001, Westminster John Knox Press.
- *Coming Out as Sacrament*, San Francisco 1998, Westminster John Knox Press.
- *The Word is Out*, San Francisco 1994
- *The Bible Reclaimed for Lesbians and Gay Men – 365 Daily Meditations*, San Francisco 1994, HarperSanFrancisco.
- *Coming Out to God: Prayers for Lesbians and Gay Men, Their Families and Friends*, Louisville 1991, Westminster John Knox Press.

Robert Goss: *Jesus Acted Up: A Gay and Lesbian Manifesto*, San Francisco 1993, Harper San Francisco.

Harry Hay: *Radically Gay: Gay Liberation in the Words of its Founder*, Boston 1996, Beacon Press.

Robert H. Hopcke: *C.G. Jung, Jungians and Homosexuality*, Boston 1989, Shambhala.

Merle James Yost: *When Love Lasts Forever: Male Couples Celebrate Commitment*, Cleveland 1999, Pilgrim Press.

Anderson Jones & David Fields: *Men Together – Portraits of Love, Commitment, and Life*, Philadelphia 1997, Running Press.

Toby Johnson: *Gay Spirituality: The Role of Gay Identity in the Transformation of Human Consciousness*, Los Angeles 2000, Alyson Books.

Winston Leyland: *Queer Dharma – Voices of Gay Buddhists*, San Francisco 1998, Gay Sunshine Press.

John J. McNeill:
- *The Church and the Homosexual*, Boston, 1976 & 1993, Beacon Press.
- *Freedom, Glorious Freedom: The Spiritual Journey to the Fullness of Life for Gays, Lesbians, and Everybody Else*, Boston 1995, Beacon Press.
- *Both Feet Firmly Planted in Midair – My Spiritual Journey*, Louisville 1998, Westminster John Knox Press.

Melanie Morrison, *The Grace of Coming Home: Spirituality, Sexuality & the Struggle for Justice*, Cleveland 1995, Pilgrim Press.

Robert Nugent: *A Challenge to Love: Gay and Lesbian Catholics in the Church*, New York 1983, Crossroad Pub Co.

Michael Seàn Paterson: *Singing for our Lives: Positively Gay & Christian*, Sheffield 1997, Cairns Publications.

Sylvia Pennington: *But Lord They're Gay: A Christian Pilgrimage*, Hawthorne 1982, Lambda Christian Fellowship.

Troy Perry: *Don't Be Afraid Anymore: The Story of Rev. Troy Perry and the Metropolitan Community Churches*, New York 1990, St Martin's Press.

Virginia Ramey Mollenkott & Letha Scanzoni: *Is the Homosexual My Neighbor? Another Christian View*, San Francisco 1980, HarperSanFrancisco.

Susan Rakoczy: *Common Journey, Different Path*, Maryknoll NY, 1992, Orbis Books.

Mary R. Ritley & L.W. Countryman: *Gifted by Otherness: Gay and Lesbian Christians in the Church*, Harrisburg, 2001, Morehouse Publishing.

Will Roscoe: *Jesus and the Shamanic Tradition of Same-Sex Love*, San Francisco 2004, Suspect Thoughts Press.

Elisabeth Stuart: *Religion is a Queer Thing: A Guide to the Christian Faith for Lesbian, Gay, Bisexual and Transgendered People*,

Cleveland 1997, Pilgrim Press.

Arlene Swidler: *Homosexuality and World Religions*, Valley Forge, 1993, Trinity Press International.

Mona West & R.E. Goss: *Take Back the Word: A Queer Reading of the Bible*, Cleveland 2000, Pilgrim Press.

Robert Williams: *Just as I am. A Practical Guide to Being Out, Proud and Christian*, New York 1992, HarperCollins.

Walter Wink (with Richard Rohr): *Homosexuality and Christian Faith*, Minneapolis 1999, Fortress Press.

Michael Vasey: *Strangers and Friends: A New Exploration of Homosexuality and the Bible*, London 1996, Hodder & Stoughton.

Addresses

The addresses and contact information listed in this chapter represent only a small selection of queer spiritual organisations available. Thanks to the internet it is now much easier to find international organisations, national caucuses or local groups. You will also encounter a lot of interesting and unexpected information just by surfing, using word combinations like 'gay spirituality', 'lesbian Christians', 'queer Buddhists', etc. Many LGB religious organisations also have links that will further help you find what you need.

A) Groups described in detail in Chapter 10:

C-QUEER - Gays and Lesbians in Christian Spirituality
C-QUEER organises retreats, seminars. Because I have moved from Switzerland to settle in the UK, C-QUEER is undergoing changes. It is my intention to continue to lead retreats, workshops, seminars whether especially for gays and lesbians or others. Some of these I will organise myself but I am also open to facilitating gatherings organised by third parties. I am also available for personal counselling.
www.friedensgasse.ch/C-Queer
Urs Mattmann ursm@bluewin.ch or umattmann@btinternet.com
The postal address and phone number of Urs Mattmann is available by request from Wild Goose Publications.

The FRIEDENSGASSE Diakonische Kommunität is a contemporary Christian order, a community of faith and life. It is rooted in the traditions of the Christian religion. It adopts an integrated spiritual approach. It is influenced by the tradition of ministry (diakonia) that has been practised since the early Christian church and it is also influenced by the ecumenical tradition.
The Friedensgasse's spiritual centre is now in Tuscany, Italy with other members currently living in Switzerland and the UK.
www.friedensgasse.ch/English
You may also contact Urs Mattmann for more information.

Metropolitan Community Church
Ecumenical Christian church especially for LGB people; many

congregations.
www.mccchurch.org (international) *and*
www.gaychurch.co.uk (Great Britain)

Lesbische und Schwule Basiskirche (LSBK)
C/O Offene Kirche Elisabethen, Elisabethenstr. 8,
CH-4051 Basel, Switzerland
Info@lsbk.ch
www.lsbk.ch
www.offenekirche.ch

Kairos in Soho
Old Compton Street, London W1V 5PA
www.kairosinsoho.org.uk
Kairos@kairos-soho.demon.co.uk

Edward Carpenter Community
BM ECC, London, WC IN 3XX
www.edwardcarpentercommunity.org.uk
Info@edwardcarpentercommunity.org.uk

Queer Spirit
3739 Balboa Street *211, San Francisco CA 94121, USA
www.qspirit.org *or*
www.revolutionarywisdom.us
Info@qspirit.org

Mercy of God Community
442 George St., New Haven, CT 06511-5411, USA
www.mgc.org

The Iona Community
Fourth Floor, Savoy House,
140 Sauchiehall Street, Glasgow G2 3DH, UK
Tel 0141 332 6343
Fax 0141 332 1090
www.iona.org.uk
ionacomm@gla.iona.org.uk

Lesbian and Gay Christian Movement
LGCM, Oxford House, Derbyshire St, London E2 6HG
Tel/Fax 020 7739 1249
www.lgcm.org.uk
lgcm@lgcm.org.uk

Kirkridge Retreat Center
2495 Fox Gap Road, Bangor, PA 18013-6028, USA
(610) 588-1793
www.kirkridge.org
kirkridge@fast.net

Easton Mountain Retreat Center
391 Herringtion Hill Road, Greenwich, NY 12834, USA
(518) 692-8023
www.Eastonmountain.org

B) Other gay and lesbian spiritual groups:

For queer evangelicals and their friends
COURAGE
PO Box 748, Guildford, GU1 2ZY, UK
www.courage.org.uk
Quaker Lesbian and Gay Fellowship QLGF
www.qlgf.org.uk

InsideOut
Inside Out was created to provide an oasis in London for gay men
to explore various aspects of wellbeing, as well as a space for
socialising in an alternative context to the 'Gay Scene'. Includes
group workshops.
www.insideoutworkshops.co.uk
info@insideoutworkshops.co.uk
Or call Khaled on 07765 094 374

REACH – Gay and Lesbian Christians
c/o Outhouse, 105 Capel Street, Dublin 1, Ireland
email: info@reachireland.net
By telephone to the Gay Switchboard Dublin 01 - 872 10 55

Julian Fellowship
Support and self-development groups for Christian lesbian women.
PO Box 5155, Dublin 14, Ireland

Quest
Gay and Lesbian Catholics
BM Box 2585, LONDON WC1N 3X
www.questgaycatholic.org.uk
quest@questgaycatholic.org.uk *or*
women@questgaycatholic.org.uk

Changing Attitudes
Working for gay and lesbian affirmation within the Anglican Church
www.changingattitude.org

Dignity USA
Lesbian, gay, bisexual & transgendered Catholics
www.dignityusa.org
dignity@aol.com

Integrity – Gay and Lesbian Episcopalians
620 Park Avenue # 311
Rochester, NY 14607-2943
Tel. 800-462-9498
www.integrityusa.org
info@integrityusa.org

Lazarus Project
A Christian spiritual project in Los Angeles, USA
www.wehopres.org/lazarusproject.html

C) Spiritual resources for gays and lesbians:

Gay Christian Networks:
www.angelfire.com/az/christiangaynet
www.gaychristians.org
www.gaychristianonline.org
www.gaychurch.org
www.inclusivechurch.net/
www.acceptingevangelicals.org

Online magazine for lesbian, gay, bisexual & transgendered Christians
www.whosoever.org

White Crane Journal
An important spiritual journal for gay men
www.whitecranejournal.com

For gay and lesbian Christians in Asia
www.QueerAsianSpirit.org

Gay Christian Networks:
www.angelfire.com/az/christiangaynet
www.gaychristians.org
www.gaychristianonline.org
www.gaychurch.org
www.inclusivechurch.net/
www.acceptingevangelicals.org

The Iona Community is:

- An ecumenical movement of men and women from different walks of life and different traditions in the Christian church
- Committed to the gospel of Jesus Christ, and to following where that leads, even into the unknown
- Engaged together, and with people of goodwill across the world, in acting, reflecting and praying for justice, peace and the integrity of creation
- Convinced that the inclusive community we seek must be embodied in the community we practise

Together with our staff, we are responsible for:

- Our islands residential centres of Iona Abbey, the MacLeod Centre on Iona, and Camas Adventure Centre on the Ross of Mull

and in Glasgow:

- The administration of the Community
- Our work with young people
- Our publishing house, Wild Goose Publications
- Our association in the revitalising of worship with the Wild Goose Resource Group

The Iona Community was founded in Glasgow in 1938 by George MacLeod, minister, visionary and prophetic witness for peace, in the context of the poverty and despair of the Depression. Its original task of rebuilding the monastic ruins of Iona Abbey became a sign of hopeful rebuilding of community in Scotland and beyond. Today, we are about 250 Members, mostly in Britain, and 1500 Associate Members, with 1400 Friends worldwide. Together and apart, 'we follow the light we have, and pray for more light'.

For information on the Iona Community contact: The Iona Community, Fourth Floor, Savoy House, 140 Sauchiehall Street, Glasgow G2 3DH, UK. Phone: 0141 332 6343
e-mail: ionacomm@gla.iona.org.uk; web: www.iona.org.uk

For enquiries about visiting Iona, please contact: Iona Abbey, Isle of Iona, Argyll PA76 6SN, UK. Phone: 01681 700404
e-mail: ionacomm@iona.org.uk

Also from Wild Goose Publications:

No Ordinary Child
A Christian mother's acceptance of her gay son
Jacqueline Ley

When Jacqueline Ley's 23-year-old son told her that he was gay, she was shocked and hurt. Her fundamentalist Christian background told her that homosexuality was sinful and that her son had placed himself beyond the pale.

One of the things that she came to learn, however, was that 'beyond the pale' is where we find Christ in the deepest and most compassionate sense; that God incarnate chose to suffer outside a city wall.

This book of reflections on a mother's journey from craving 'normality' for her child to celebrating him as a blessedly extraordinary creature of God is not only a chronicle of a remarkable change of attitude. It is also an argument for letting go of our preconceptions about other people – often those nearest and dearest to us – and acknowledging that what God plans for their lives may be something greater and more mysterious than we can ever imagine.

ISBN 1 901557 61 8

For full details of all our publications
and online ordering:
www.ionabooks.com